CATCH A FLORIDA KEYS GRAND SLAM

A CONSERVATIONIST'S GUIDE TO ONE OF FISHING'S GREATEST ACHIEVEMENTS

THOMPSON SMITH

Copyright © 2022 Thompson Smith. All rights reserved.

The content contained within this book may not be reproduced, duplicated, or transmitted without direct written permission from the author or the publisher.

Under no circumstances will any blame or legal responsibility be held against the publisher or author for any damages, reparation, or monetary loss due to the information contained within this book, either directly or indirectly.

Legal Notice:

This book is copyright-protected. It is only for personal use. You cannot amend, distribute, sell, use, quote, or paraphrase any part of the content within this book without the consent of the author or publisher.

Disclaimer Notice:

Please note that the information contained within this document is for educational and entertainment purposes only. All effort has been executed to present accurate, up-to-date, reliable, and complete information. No warranties of any kind are declared or implied. Readers acknowledge that the author is not engaged in the rendering of legal, financial, medical, or professional advice. The content within this book has been derived from various sources. Please consult a licensed professional before attempting any techniques outlined in this book.

By reading this document, the reader agrees that under no circumstances is the author responsible for any losses, direct or indirect, that are incurred as a result of the use of the information contained within this document, including, but not limited to, errors, omissions, or inaccuracies.

CONTENTS

Introduction	7
1. LET'S GET GOING! 15	
The Upper Keys	16

Middle Keys	19
Lower Keys	20
2. PLANNING YOUR TRIP 25	
How Long to Stay	26
What to Bring	26
3. CHOOSING YOUR GUIDE 33	
Some History	33
Half Day Charters	38
Three Quarter Day Charters	39
Full Day Charters	40
Specialty Charters	41
My Experience	42
4. UPPER AND MIDDLE KEYS 47	
Upper Keys	47
Middle Keys	54
5. LOWER KEYS 59	
Big Pine Key	61
Torch Keys	65
Cudjoe Key	71
Sugarloaf Key	77
Key West	96
6. CONSERVATION 105	
Leading Associations	105
Best Practices	109

7. HABITAT PRESERVATION	113	
Tarpon Habitat		115
Bonefish Spawning		116
Project Permit		117
8. SHARK DEPREDATION	121	
Conclusion		125
Resources		131
Acknowledgments		133

In loving memory of my father, who always made time to take his family fishing.

INTRODUCTION

"He's coming in at 1:00 at 50 feet, further to the right, further…that's it, take your shot!"

The wind was coming in straight from the North, and I knew I would have to give it my all to get the crab in front of the fish with just 6lb test. So, I cast out with everything I had, and just as I let it go, a cool gust of North wind caught my crab and blew it ten feet off target.

"Again, again," pleaded Captain Tim in a nervous voice. I reeled up the crab and, at that point, had lost sight of "The Man."

"I lost him, Capt."

"He is going across the bow now at 30ft to your left, see him?"

"No, sir," I answered back in a tense whisper.

"Point your rod," Capt. Tim urged. "Left, left…11:00 o'clock…got him?"

"YES! I see him," and I sent the crab into the air and watched as it dropped perfectly five feet in front of the permit.

"Leave it, leave it," yelled Capt. Tim, I could see the fish turn toward my crab as the captain yelled, "Twitch it, twitch it." As I did, the fish turned sideways to the skiff, showing us his magnificent flat silver side. He was big. With one mighty sweep of his powerful forked tail, the fish lunged forward and, in a puff of sand, swallowed the crab and turned away. I felt the heavy weight against my rod and wound down as I lifted it to set the hook. In a split second, the 6lb line started screaming off the reel as the magnificent fish took off.

"Get your rod tip up," yelled Capt. Tim, as the permit took off across the flat. After fishing for many years with Tim, I knew what to do, but in the moment at the precipice of achieving one of fishing's greatest accomplishments, emotions run high.

"I got it…I got it," I yelled back, but the fish screamed off.

Again, Tim yelled, "He is heading for the channel; I'm going to start the motor. Just keep your rod above your head. There is coral everywhere!"

From the top of the casting platform, I could see the fish clearly heading off the flat and toward the safety of the deep channel. Capt. Tim was making up ground as I wound furiously to get my line back and keep the angle of the line high to minimize the chance of it getting caught up in the coral.

"He is 25lbs plus!" yelled Captain Tim as we motored straight into the wind, creating a chill in the air on this April afternoon, in the backcountry behind Sugarloaf Key.

"I can't turn him, Capt., I'm afraid to put too much pressure on him. Damn, he is strong!"

"You're doing great," Tim responded. "We've got some time before he gets to the channel, but let's run up to his side to change the angle and hopefully get him to stay on the flat." Tim was able to speed up the skiff, and as he did, I was able to get more line back and change the angle of pressure. The fish was only 10 yards away now. "Okay, now you can put a little more pressure on him," Tim said. "Lower the rod and pull to the side." I did, and the fish slowly turned his head and headed away from the channel.

"I turned him, Capt!" As the words left my mouth, the magnificent permit, dubbed "The Man," saw the boat and turned away, ripping off 50 yards of line in 3 seconds. He went over the ledge into the channel, and POP, he was gone.

It was mid-April in 1980, and I was on spring break from photography studies at the Florida Institute of Technology in Jensen Beach, Florida. My father had come down from Virginia Beach to visit the Keys, where he served our country in the Navy during the Cuban Missile Crisis in the 60s. He had been bringing my family and me on vacation to the Keys for many years. We actually lived in Key West for a couple of years before he moved us back to Virginia. Fishing the backcountry for tarpon, bonefish, and permit was a passion for him, and it became one for me as well. I caught my first bonefish when I was twelve and even held a Junior Florida State Record for tarpon as a fourteen-year-old, one hundred thirty-one pounds on thirty-pound test.

This day would become very special because it was the first time I heard the term "Grand Slam" in fishing.

> We left Sugarloaf Marina that morning. It was going to be a day of flats fishing for bonefish with my dad and longtime guide and family friend Captain Tim Carlile. We headed to the backcountry along a beautiful winding creek through the

mangroves—lush, dense, and full of life. As Tim navigated the creek full of mangrove roots that reached out to grab the boat, we glided across the glassy water. Suddenly, he slowed down and told me to grab the rod with the white bucktail. He had spotted a small school of tarpon rolling ahead of the boat. He slowed the boat to a crawl and cut the motor, so we were floating in silence.

"Right there," my father whispered, pointing to the mangroves, and there they were sipping air as they rolled on the surface. I threw out my bucktail and let it sink slowly just in front of the fish, and as I began to retrieve the lure, one grabbed it and took to the air in a magnificent leap. As he did, he threw the hook.

"What didn't you do, Thompson?" asked Capt. Tim.

"I don't know, it happened so fast," I replied.

"You have to bow to the King, remember?"

"Of course, damn!"

You have to give slack to your line when a tarpon jumps by "bowing" your rod toward them when they are in the air, relieving tension. In my haste, I had forgotten.

"They are still here. Let's get back in there," said Capt. Tim. He moved the boat forward, and soon we had the school in our sights. After a few misplaced casts, I found my mark and had a nice twenty-pound fish at boatside—a nice bonus to a day of bonefishing. We quickly headed out to the bonefish flats because the tide was going out, and the water would be perfect for spotting "tailing bones" foraging for shrimp.

When we arrived on the flat, it was my father's turn to be on the casting platform, and as we scoured the flat, we saw a large school of about twenty ahead of us. At first, they were out of casting range. Capt. Tim quickly and quietly polled the boat into position to give my father a shot. After so many years of experience, his first cast was perfect. Watching him spot the fish, crouch to hide, let the cast go, and land his shrimp perfectly always amazed me. He was on! On this beautiful spring day, the fish were plentiful, and it wasn't long before I had a bonefish to the boat as well.

"Well, you know what this means," Tim said to my father.

"Yes, I do."

In unison, they said, "GRAND SLAM!"

I didn't know what they were talking about at the time, but this day would change my life forever. The International Game Fish Association acknowledges many Grand Slams—catching three different game fish in the same calendar day. From freshwater bass and trout to saltwater billfish and tuna, any three game fish caught by the same angler count. However, one of the most recognized and prized is the Florida Keys Grand Slam—a tarpon, bonefish, and permit all in the same day. Very difficult to accomplish, this feat requires planning, timing, and luck. In this book, I am going to give you all the tools you will need to have the best opportunity. This will put you in position to clinch your Grand Slam, but you must make your own luck!

As described in the short story above, I have been heartbroken in the pursuit of a Grand Slam since I was nineteen years old. To this day, I have not yet accomplished the feat, and I am sixty years old. So many are the stories from, not only the Keys, but around the world. I have had surfing and fishing adventures in Mexico, Costa Rica, Panama, Nicaragua, the South Pacific, and the Caribbean, as well as freshwater adventures in Montana, Idaho, New Mexico, and Wyoming. I have experienced a lot of successes and frustrations. Having said that, I wouldn't change a thing because it is the passion of the pursuit and the people that accompany you that make this challenge so special. I have been able to gain an understanding, through the years, that the journey to accomplish something very difficult can be one the most rewarding challenges.

In this book and future books to follow, you will find information that I have gathered throughout the years to guide you to successfully achieve your Grand Slam. I will also be sharing some personal experiences that might make your journey a little bit easier and more fun!

Tight lines,

Thompson

1

LET'S GET GOING!

So here you are taking your first steps to planning the trip of a lifetime to accomplish one of fishing's greatest achievements…the Grand Slam. You've seen the videos, heard the stories, done some research, and now you are giving me the chance to share over forty years of knowledge chasing this dream. In the chapters to follow, you will get specific information on when, with whom, and how to get your Grand Slam, but I want to first set the scene for what you can expect on this journey.

The Florida Keys are one of the most beautiful island chains with one of the most diverse ecosystems in the country, if not the world. From the mangrove forest in the back country to the stunning coral reefs of the Atlantic, the Keys offer the curious adventurer a chance to expand their experiences and enrich their lives. On this trip, you and your family are going to see some of the most beautiful water, unique birdlife, the famous key deer, and insanely beautiful sunsets!

Whether you are going to the Upper, Middle, or Lower Keys, I recommend you fly into Miami Airport and rent a car to enjoy the rest of your drive. This allows you time to acclimate after your long flight. You can leave the airport, get in the car, roll the windows down, and feel the warm Florida air as you get out of town and onto the Ronald Regan Turnpike. Go through Homestead and Florida City and head into the southern part of the Everglades National Park. You will feel your heart rate slow as you pass Manatee Bay to the north and Blackwater Sound to the south. Time will start to slow down as you see Key Largo in the distance. If you are traveling with children, this is when the questions will begin as the landscape turns from the mainland to the islands. Your spouse will probably have their arm out the window doing that "wind surfing" thing with their hand as the warm air fills your senses.

THE UPPER KEYS

As you drive along the Overseas Highway, take note of the mile markers. They give your distance from Key West as well as point out landmarks along your journey. Mile marker 106 is where the Key Largo Chamber of Commerce is located. There are several guides you can bookmark on your phone noting historical points of interest, restaurants, lodging, campgrounds, marinas, parks and beaches, boat ramps, kayak launches, and things to do in the Florida Keys. This is a fun thing for your trip's navigator to have, so they can see what is coming up!

Your first main attraction on Key Largo will be John Pennekamp Coral Reef State Park, and if you are staying in the Upper or even the Middle Keys, this is a must-see snorkeling and diving location. As your road trip continues, you will come up on Tavernier Key, which has a rich fishing history. This very laid-back Key is worth slowing down to see. We are now in the middle of Florida Bay and really getting into the island chain proper. Where the water starts to turn from a clear, crystal green to a beautiful turquoise, and the water becomes crystal clear!

Whether you have kids or not, the Blond Giraffe Key Lime Pie Factory is a must-stop to stretch your legs and sink deeper into "Keys Time." Not only do they have some of the best Key Lime pie (and many other goodies), but they have also created a wonderful atmosphere.

A serenity garden—sorry, no dogs, a groovy soundtrack, and a classic tropical atmosphere welcome you to your journey. You may not realize it yet, but at this point, the city is so far behind you that it is time to bring out the tropical clothing gear!

As you leave Tavernier Key, you cross one of the 42 bridges along the Overseas Highway. Here, you can see both the Florida Bay to your right and the Atlantic Ocean on the left. The bridge crosses Tavernier Creek which is one of many creeks that connect these two bodies of water and the Gulf of Mexico. As we head further south, the next Key that is important on your journey is Islamorada, "The Sportfishing Capital of the World." Now your mind can flip that switch and turn your whole focus to fishing as you come up to the famous Bud n' Mary's Marina. Pull into the marina to stretch your legs and check in to see what's biting. There is nothing better than talking with the folks at the tackle shop, and hopefully a captain or two, about what is happening out on the water. Bud n' Mary's does a lot of offshore fishing, but it doesn't end there. With some of the best guides in the industry, the backcountry fishing here is some of the best in the world.

The excitement of getting out on the water and pursuing your Grand Slam continues to grow as you get back on the road and pass between Upper and Lower Matecumbe Keys. This stretch of the Overseas Highway is one of the most beautiful examples of the environment in which bonefish, tarpon, and permit live. Teatable Key Channel, Indian Key Channel, and Lignumvitae Channel are three classic deep channels where tarpon congregate, surrounded by pristine flats and where bonefish and permit lurk, looking for shrimp, crabs, and small fish. Now, to really get your blood pumping, make sure to stop in at Robbie's Marina on the right as you pass over Lignumvitae Channel (you can't miss it) to feed the tarpon and have an adult beverage! This popular spot really allows you to chat with other visitors and dive deeper into the tropical feel of the islands, as you get ready to leave the Upper Keys for the Middle Keys.

MIDDLE KEYS

This next leg of your journey will fill your senses with "Keys Fever," as you get into the heart of the Keys. The bridges are getting longer over the deep turquoise water, starting with the Channel #2 bridge, which takes you past Craig Key, and the Channel #5 bridge, which takes you to Long Key. There is great fishing along the Overseas Heritage Trail, which parallels the drive, with many platforms to fish from. These areas boast great bottom fishing for snapper, small grouper, and others.

Coming up on Vaca Key, Aquarium Encounters is a fun stop for adults and children alike. It is a marine park with lots of things to do, including a snorkeling adventure in their private lagoon!

Marathon Key is your next major destination. This mecca for many fishermen allows you to maximize your time on the water due to its easy access to both the Gulf and the Atlantic. This is a great place to try for your Grand Slam!

LOWER KEYS

After Marathon, you cross into the Lower Keys via the Seven Mile Bridge. This is an amazing experience on your drive, as you seemingly glide over the pristine waters for, well, seven miles! The original Seven Mile Bridge now called the Old Seven Mile Bridge, or "Old Seven," runs parallel to the modern structure. The two structures, weathered by salt spray, are recognized throughout the world as the symbol of the Keys.

Enduring the battering of numerous hurricanes, the two bridges represent the enduring spirit of the Keys' residents.

The modern-day bridge, opened to traffic in 1982, is one of the world's longest segmental bridges at 6.79 miles (or nearly 36,000 feet) long. A 65-foot-high clearance allows boat passage between the Gulf of Mexico and the Atlantic Ocean. The Old Bridge has been restored and has reopened for pedestrian traffic to Pigeon Key. This restored bridge is a living portion of Henry Flagler's original Overseas Highway. Pigeon Key is a historical landmark and a big part of the rich history of the Florida Keys. You can feel the island's serenity and soak it in by touring the former section-guards' quarters, former paint foreman's dorm, and museum while gazing upon the modern new structure that leads you down to the Lower Keys. The two bridges stand resolutely as an enduring legacy to Flagler, the persevering dreamer who envisioned what the Keys could be. It is a 4.4-mile round-trip walk along the side of the Overseas Highway, over some of the most beautiful waterscapes you will ever see.

Just over halfway on the bridge, make sure to wave at Donna the Bush and Fred the Tree, an Australian pine tree that defies nature by growing right out of the bridge! On the South side of the bridge is Bahia Honda Key and the Bahia Honda State Park, where you will find a quiet beach and camping site along the old railroad bridge. This railroad bridge was permanently damaged by a hurricane in 1935, but the area is still known for being a major thoroughfare during the tarpon migration each year. During the palolo worm hatch, massive schools of tarpon descend on this area— as well as lots of fishermen! Conservationists are pushing to limit the number of fishermen allowed into this area during the hatch, which only lasts about two weeks in late May or early June, to relieve pressure on the fish and allow them to enjoy this feeding event naturally.

Crossing the Spanish Harbor Channel, you will be entering my favorite part of the Lower Keys, not only for fishing but for the wildlife as well. From Big Pine down to Big Coppitt Key, there is such a diverse amount of wildlife. It is well worth it to spend some time looking for birdlife, reptiles, and the famous key deer. Just past the nature center on Big Pine, turn right on the road to the Blue Hole Observation Platform. As you cruise along through the heart of Big Pine, you are pretty much guaranteed to see the key deer. Also on Big Pine is a wonderful little place to load up on good food for the rest of your road trip. The Good Food Conspiracy is a brightly colored health food grocery store and juice bar that also has a deli right on the Overseas Highway. The walls are lined with an extensive selection of vitamins, supplements, and herbs. The fridges are filled with healthy cold drinks and snacks, and have a great selection of dried fruits and nuts. The baking section is full of hard-to-find ancient grains, flours, baking supplies, and more.

The stretch of the Overseas Highway that goes between Big Pine and Lower Sugarloaf Key crosses some of the best fishing waters in the world. From Little Torch, Ramrod, Summerland,

and Cudjoe to Upper and Lower Sugarloaf Keys, this area has some of the most pristine fishing waters I have ever seen. I have traveled here as a boy, a teenager, a young man, and as a fishing-crazed adult, and every time I get to this area, I feel fulfilled. This area was hit hard by Hurricane Irma in 2017, but the resilient "Conchs" of the Lower Keys have restored this beautiful area as they have for generations. Now, it is off to Key West!

The last part of your drive will take you past the Naval Air Station on Boca Chica, on to Stock Island, and finally ending in Key West. "The Conch Republic," as it is known to the locals, is not only an amazing fishing destination, but for those seeking a more festive fishing experience, this is the place! World-renowned restaurants, a fascinating nightlife, and a great art scene make Key West a perfect destination for the fisherman who also enjoys a great, eclectic party scene. It is also very family-friendly.

I hope you enjoyed this mental road trip and are now even more excited, as I am, to figure out where to park yourself and get serious about what you came here for —your Grand Slam. "The Gray Ghost of the Flats" (bonefish), "The Man" (permit), and, of course, "The Silver King" (tarpon) are waiting for you. So, let's get after it!

2

PLANNING YOUR TRIP

A key factor in planning your trip is whether you are going to trailer a boat down to the Keys or if you are going to hire a guide to help you on your quest. Both options are viable, but for the sake of brevity, I am going to focus on the latter, as your chances of success are much greater with an experienced guide. Having said that, if you are a seasoned angler and have logged many hours on the water, there will be plenty of information here to give you a better chance at catching your Slam. Whether you are using conventional tackle or fly fishing, there will be general information about locations, bait, and artificials, as well as times of the year to get you in the best spots at the best times to get you on the fish.

HOW LONG TO STAY

As I demonstrated in chapter one, there are three areas of the Keys—Upper, Middle, and Lower. All three give you great opportunities to catch your Grand Slam and should be considered in your trip planning. It just depends on your budget and time, of course, to decide where you want to go. For shorter trips of 2-3 days, consider the Upper Keys if you are driving. If you are flying, however, you can fly right into Marathon or Key West if you want to reach the Middle or Lower Keys. Mid-length trips of 3-5 days give you more options of either covering more water or getting one location dialed in. Of course, longer trips of 7-10 days or more give you the best opportunity and the most options, if your budget allows.

WHAT TO BRING

Whether you are going it on your own or hiring a guide, you will need sun protection and mosquito repellent. You are going to be in warm, humid environments where mosquitoes thrive. There are plenty of other pests as well, but mosquitoes are the biggest nuisance. I was once fishing out of Islamorada, in the backcountry amongst the mangroves, looking for small tarpon. It was late May in 2002, and I did not come fully prepared for these annoying little buggers. As the sun went down and the fishing turned on, so did the mosquitoes. They got so bad that I was forced to stop fishing and leave! Of course, now we have much better protective clothing: lightweight long-sleeve shirts with SPF 50 built in, buffs to protect your face, gloves, and lightweight long pants. All are worth the investment to keep you on the water, especially at the Golden Hour. There are also great products for your skin now, as well, if you don't want to wear long clothing. I know some anglers, especially some of the fly guys, who feel like their movement is constricted with this apparel. So, investigate and find what works best for you.

If you are going to be fishing with a guide, they all have the tackle you will need for either conventional spinning or fly fishing. If you are bringing your own, for bonefish, choose lightweight spinning gear from 6 lb to 12 lb or 6-8 wt for fly rods. For permit, bring medium spin for 12-20 lb or the same fly gear (6-8wt). For tarpon, you need heavier gear, 15-30 lb for spinning and 8-10wt for fly rods.

Line choice is one of constant debate. The newer braided lines that are currently the buzz of the fishing world offer a strong line with a smaller diameter, allowing for more reel capacity. They come in a variety of colors designed to be less visible to fish, but research has shown that some fish can sense and then shy away from them. Classic monofilament lines have some drawbacks. They do stretch, and their thicker diameter keeps reel capacity down. However, they have been proven effective over the years. As far as terminal tackle and lures go, there are so many options for you to consider. I won't go into that in great detail here. There are Facebook pages where anglers share information as to what they use, and of course, you can check with your local tackle shop or call tackle shops in the area you will be fishing for their advice. These are just guidelines, and your choice depends on what kind of challenge you want for yourself. Whatever type of gear you choose, make sure it is in tip-top shape. The conditions in the Keys are brutal on tackle, so to guarantee the best chances for success, all gear must be ready to go.

This type of fishing is mainly done by sight casting to your target, so I can't emphasize the importance of a high-quality pair of polarized sunglasses enough. Even with these, it is extremely difficult to spot the fish. I can't tell you how many times my guide has spotted fish and called out the location and distance, only to be frustrated by my inability to see. They would yell, "Just throw it!" Of course, that was just blind casting and not my best chance to hook up. It has taken me years to be able to determine what is a fish and what is not on the flats and to see when the fish has taken my bait or fly. Having a good pair of wrap-around polarized sunglasses to block out as much side glare as possible will increase your odds of spotting fish tremendously. They are well worth the investment.

When I was younger, I became obsessed with wading the flats after watching many shows about bonefishing in the Bahamas, where they would wade the flats all afternoon chasing bones. When I was thirteen years old, I spent three weeks on Sugarloaf Key working for Captain Cliff Carlile. I helped with harvesting sponges, helped tickle up some bugs (during commercial lobster season), cleaned up around the docks, and just be a pain in the ass to the captains. Instead of getting paid, once the captains and specifically Cliff's son, Captain Tim, got done with his day, we would run out to the flats and enjoy an evening wade for bones. This was a rite of passage that, to this day, I cherish very much.

We went out to the flats one evening with Pepe and Capt. Tim, and when Tim found just the right spot to anchor up, we spotted a school of bones tailing about 60 yards away. We got our 6lb spinning gear set up with live shrimp and slowly eased ourselves into the water, so as not to spook the fish. Back then, in 1974, we went in barefoot, and if you didn't have "Keys Feet", the turtle grass, sponges, and coral made it difficult to maintain your focus on the fish, to say the least.

At this point, I had been out with the guys three times before and had yet to land my first bone. We spread out about 50 feet apart and, as quietly as we could, started heading towards the fish. The warm water was only about knee deep, and we had to crouch over to keep a low profile. Remember, flats fishing is just as much hunting and stalking as it is fishing, so keeping yourself between the fish and the sun is important to keep that low profile, as the fish are very spooky in such shallow conditions. With tails glistening in the evening light, the fish were heads down and actively feeding. A group of three fish moved off from the pack and were heading right for me. Once they were within casting range, I took my rod to my side and softly sidearmed my shrimp into the group. I held my breath as I watched the shrimp fly through the air. When I realized it might be too close, I stopped the line from going out with my left hand and raised the rod tip with my right. The shrimp landed with a splash right on the nose of the lead fish and spooked them. The group dashed off but quickly circled back. I was standing as still as a statue when I saw one of the bones moving right in line with my shrimp. I slowly lifted the shrimp, as it had started to bury itself in the sand, and the fish saw it and darted in for the bait. BAM! He ate it, and I set the hook, lifting my rod high above my head. I couldn't help but scream, "Fish on!" to the guys.

Tim yelled back, "Good job, Tee" (my nickname). The fish took off, and I soon found myself watching line melt off the reel. Purely on instinct, I took off running across the flat. I could feel chunks of coral hitting my heels and turtle grass cutting between my toes, and by the time I caught up with the fish, I could see blood coming from my feet.

I tell you this story to make a point. If you are going to try wading the flats, a good pair of wading boots or shoes will keep your feet protected. Simms, Orvis, and Pelagic all have great options. Wading the flats really is a wonderful way to hunt for these fish, so if you are with a guide, let them know that this is something you are interested in doing. I'm sure they will be happy to get you into the water.

One of the most important things to bring with you on your quest to catch a Grand Slam is patience. No matter how long your trip will be, you will be tested. For experienced anglers, this is not a news flash. Frustration is part of this game, so be ready for it. Permit especially can wreak havoc on your patience. It may take you hours just to spot one, and even the best guides, the best spot, and your best cast is just where the game begins. Tarpon are just plain strong. Thrown hooks, broken leaders, and tackle-busting jumps will test your will. Bonefish are so hard to see, with their perfect camouflage, that you might not even see one until it is right up on the boat, and then it is too late. They will spook and be gone before you can even say, "There's one!" Even with all of these frustrations, it is the challenge that makes this experience so special, and at the end of the day, you will have some great stories!

3

CHOOSING YOUR GUIDE

There are literally hundreds of guides to choose from in the Keys, so this can be a daunting process and choice. Of course, narrowing them down to the region you will be fishing is the first step, and I will touch on that in upcoming chapters. Understanding the history of guiding in the Keys will give you a better understanding of what to expect during your search.

SOME HISTORY

Offshore fishing was popular back in the 1920s. It wasn't until the 1930s, with famed angler Zane Grey, that fishing the backcountry for tarpon gained momentum. Finally, in the late 1940s and early 1950s, sight fishing for bonefish, permit, and tarpon became popular. There were very few visiting anglers coming down to the Keys at that time, and guides had to supplement their income by lobstering and sponging. In 1956, a group of pioneering guides started a fishing conservation organization on Islamorada called the Islamorada Fishing Guides Association, which was renamed to the Florida Keys Fishing Guides Association (FKFGA) in 1979.

The first order of business for the organization in 1956 was to make sure all members had a U.S. Coast Guard Captain's License. The second was for them to make sure they could take care of themselves. There was no Coast Guard in the Keys at that time, and of course, no radios or cell phones were handy. So, they had to look out for each other. Much of the fishing in those days was done within a mile of the shoreline; each year, the guides would go further into the Everglades National Park. The distance required them to keep track of each other, and no guide left the dock for home until all were accounted for.

The guides met monthly to go over safety issues, fishing etiquette, and, of course, any conflicts amongst themselves. Only a handful of the guides were able to stay busy enough making $25 per day. A couple of the guides were able to entice anglers from the Miami Rod and Reel Club to come down and challenge themselves with the big tarpon, but other guides struggled to find clients. In the 1960s, things changed as baseball star Ted Williams grew interested in the Keys' fisheries and visited frequently, boosting publicity to the area. During that time, the FKFGA developed the Islamorada Gold Cup Tarpon Championship, and the rules established the catch-and-release philosophy, which is now the core of the organization. The tournament attracted many anglers to the Keys, and consequently, the number of guides joining increased. Now, the guides were making $75 per day!

Commercial fishing was increasing as well, and this put a strain on the fishery. Mullet populations declined, and bonefish and redfish were being killed in the commercial nets. The eel grass was dying from a decrease in freshwater flows. The organization knew it had to have a stronger voice in the Everglades National Park and the Florida Marine Fisheries Commission. In December of 1976, the FKFGA held a general meeting to discuss what the organization was going to do, and this was the beginning of the move toward conservation.

The organization went to work immediately on banning commercial netting in the Everglades National Park and reducing daily bag limits for backcountry fish.

In 1978, the members agreed to further reduce bag limits and not to sell fish from charters. With a membership of over 200, their voices were being heard, and conservation was the key topic. In 1980, the National Park Service announced that commercial netting would be phased out of the Park over five years, never to be reinstated. Additional good news continued as bag limits were lowered again, and personal watercraft and the harvesting of lobster within the park were banned. The FKFGA also played a major role in how shrimp are harvested from bridges, helping to eliminate the amount of bycatch.

The FKFGA never stopped protesting the killing of tarpon, and many guides refused to guide in tournaments that allowed it. The organization made a huge impact on attitudes, and in 1986, the Don Hawley Tarpon Tournament became a catch-and-release-only tournament, followed by the Gold Cup in 1993. It was not until 1995 that any killed tarpon required a permit to be legal. FKFGA members are very active on many boards and committees of the Florida Keys National Marine Sanctuary. They have recommended noncombustible motor zones, which help to protect the flats and wild bird habitat, and they raised substantial funds for the Wild Bird Center to help with birds that are hurt from fishing lines.

In 1990, the organization started an all-release bonefish, snook, and redfish tournament called the Swamp Guides Ball to raise funds for guides in need of financial assistance. This has grown to be one of the most popular tournaments, raising over $300,000 for the Guides Trust Foundation. The organization has stayed busy with limiting bag numbers, seagrass replenishment, catch and release, no kill policies, kids' programs, as well as staying active on numerous boards and committees.

The guide community has a long history, and many of the guides you will be contacting are active members, ensuring that their fisheries are protected. Most are happy to tell you about it. A lot of the guides we will talk about have been actively guiding in the Keys for most of their lives, beginning as teenagers. The best guides are very difficult to book; unfortunately, some have a one-year waiting list, and others are just not taking on new clients. There are guides that book over 350 charters a year! Don't let this discourage you. There are plenty of young and upcoming guides that are eager to take you out on the water and catch that Slam!

Choosing one of these younger guides is an opportunity for you to establish a long-term relationship that will allow you to hone your skills alongside them. I started fishing in the Keys with my father in 1971, at ten years old. We fished with one of his Navy buddies, Captain Cliff Carlisle, on Sugarloaf Key. As previously mentioned, Cliff's son Tim began guiding there as well during his teenage years. Cliff was mainly an ocean guide, and Tim focused on the backcountry. We established lifelong friendships with this family through fishing that we keep to this day. All the young guides you will find today have been mentored by the great guides of the past. They have put in countless hours on the water to sharpen their skills and help you have the fishing day of your dreams.

Pricing for guide services in the Keys is pretty consistent thanks to the FKFGA, but you will see some fluctuation based on how many years they have been guiding. Also, keep in mind if you are fishing on your own, anyone over 16 will need to secure a Florida fishing license. If you are going with a guide, licenses are included in the day rate.

HALF DAY CHARTERS

If your time is short or you want to do more than just spend the day on the water, a half-day charter is the most economical way to get out and try your luck. Backcountry trips for two anglers pay an average of $500 plus gratuity. If you have a third angler, add $100.

Half-day trips, typically 4 hours, are good for the experienced angler taking their daughter or son out for the first time. Of course, this length of trip makes it difficult to complete a Grand Slam, but it has been done before. More than likely, you will have a chance to catch two species, probably bonefish and baby tarpon, on a half day, with the possibility of snapper, jacks, snook, and redfish. It is usually a bit of a stretch to reach permit grounds, depending on where you are fishing, on a half-day trip.

THREE QUARTER DAY CHARTERS

These 6-hour charters average $600 plus gratuity for two people. Add $100 for a third, and of course, this increases your chances of completing a Grand Slam. Having an extra two hours on the water allows you to experience a tidal change, which can increase your chances of seeing both bonefish and permit. These two hours may also give you the opportunity to see tarpon in the channels on the incoming tide as well as the flats, increasing your opportunities. Three-quarter day trips offer you a great opportunity to maximize your time on the water, while also leaving you some daylight hours. This is especially important if you want to explore the Lower Keys or Key West.

FULL DAY CHARTERS

For the maximum experience and the best odds to catch your Grand Slam, a full-day charter is the best choice. Depending on the time of year, full days can be from 8 to 10 hours and average $800 - $900 plus gratuity for two people (add $100 for a third). Most guides will tell you that this length of trip gives them the time to make sure you have multiple opportunities for each species. This, of course, gives you more chances to hook fish, therefore increasing your chances of landing them. Keep in mind, you may get two or three tarpon in the morning, maybe see a half a dozen bonefish in the midday, and then hopefully see a few permit in the afternoon hours.

The luxury of this much time with your guide may (no promises) give you the opportunity to experience one of the greatest and simplest culinary experiences of your life. Some of the guides in the Keys also fish for stone crab and lobster throughout the year. If you're lucky, they may pull one of their traps with you and take you to the backcountry, start a fire, and boil up one of these delicacies for your lunch. There is nothing, and I mean nothing, like a cold beer (which you will also use to cook with) and your fresh shellfish seasoned with Old Bay and hot sauce, enjoyed on an uninhabited Key, on a pristine beach—perfection!

Full-day charters allow you to really get to know your guide, which in turn will give you the opportunity to see how devoted, knowledgeable, skilled, and passionate they are about their craft. Humor, sarcasm, and even a bit of tough love will all be a part of your day. The guides in the Keys are some of the best in the world, and the amount of time spent on the water with these men and women is priceless. The endless stories of trials and tribulations will keep you entertained during any downtime. You will probably laugh harder at some of the tales you hear this day than at any other time in your life. Hopefully, your story will be one they tell in the future, and that story will be of how you got your Grand Slam!

SPECIALTY CHARTERS

There are a variety of specialty charters in the Keys, including sightseeing, snorkeling, and nature viewing. For the fisherman, there is a 4-hour night tarpon trip. This unique trip puts you on the tarpon during their peak feeding time and is a very exciting experience. Although this is specifically to catch a tarpon at night, it is a fun way to help get your Grand Slam if you don't get it during your day charter. The trips are for two anglers and average $500 plus gratuity. Usually done in or around the bridges of the Overseas Highway, these trips are usually live bait trips. There are a variety of live baits that work well, including pilchards, pinfish, grunts, and probably the most effective mullet. With the boat anchored up current from the structures, the baits are usually "fly-lined" out, so they can free swim. Some baits may be put down to the bottom to make sure the water column is covered. This type of fishing is very exciting, especially when you see the mullet start to jump in the air to escape the tarpon circling below. There is usually a light on the boat focused on the water and some ambient light from the bridges. When the water explodes with the feeding frenzy, you will see a beautiful sight as the silver sides of the tarpon shine in the night. In the still of the night, you can even hear the gill plates clacking as the tarpon jumps from the water, shaking its head side to side!

MY EXPERIENCE

After finishing my senior project for my photography degree at FIT, I needed a break. I convinced my girlfriend to take a road trip down to the Keys, specifically to night fish for tarpon. South Florida and the Keys are very hot during the summer, so fishing at night is pleasant. Being on a college student budget, we decided to camp at Bahia Honda State Park and try our luck from the bridge. After getting the camp set up that evening, we walked through the campgrounds talking to other campers who we could see had been fishing. Most were just bottom fishing for snapper and grouper, but one couple had been looking for tarpon. They said they had seen tarpon during the day, but they weren't actively feeding. I told them I had some experience in night fishing for tarpon, and we should try going together the next evening. So, we made plans to go after dinner the next night.

In the morning, I set out to get bait for that night. Although chunk bait, like mullet and ballyhoo, can be effective for tarpon at night, live bait is the way to go, so I set off to catch some pinfish. Now, if you have small children with you, this is a fun activity for them. Using very light spinning tackle, small hooks, and small pieces of shrimp for bait, you can keep the kids happy for hours catching pinfish. Around the campground, there are several areas to target these little guys, and you will probably get some small snapper as well. The docks by the RV camp area are a great place to start the day. It is important to remember that you are going to need to keep your bait alive for the day, and the best way to do that is with a bait bucket equipped with an aerator. Marine Metal has one on Amazon for $25.00.

I headed down to the docks, and it wasn't long before I had a bucket full of pinfish. I decided to go back to camp for the day and rest up for the night's fishing. My girlfriend had never caught a tarpon, so I was excited for her to have this opportunity. We had done many night fishing trips near campus, in Jensen Beach, for snook and seen tarpon, but this was her first trip specifically for the Silver King. We spent the afternoon preparing our gear and talking strategy, and we were getting very excited as the sun slipped below the horizon. We went off to meet our new friends and found ourselves at the water's edge, just below the Old Train Bridge. There is a nice bulkhead here within casting distance of a small channel that tarpon use to get between the ocean and the Gulf. It is not a deep channel, but the access is good with enough room to spread out.

It was a clear, beautiful night, and the stars were out putting on a show. Bahia Honda is the darkest part of the Keys, providing some of the best stargazing you can find. Unaffected by light pollution, this area is a gathering spot for people to learn about the constellations and just enjoy the beauty of the universe. However, we had fishing to do, so we got our baits in the water and settled in for a fun night. It was a very quiet night with hardly any other people around, so we heard every little sound. Before we knew it, we could hear tarpon in the near distance rolling slowly in the channel, slurping for air. Our excitement level grew as our friends' rod bent, and they were hooked up! Unfortunately, the fight was short-lived as a barracuda jumped at the end of the line, cutting them off with its razor-sharp teeth. We quickly re-rigged their line and got another live pinfish back out into the channel. An hour or so passed without hearing any more tarpon, but in that time, we caught a few nice-sized mangrove snapper to fill the cooler for fish sandwiches the next day.

Time was passing quickly, and our friends decided to call it an evening. We said our goodbyes and planned to catch up the next day. My girlfriend was determined to stay, as was I, to see if we could get just one good chance at a nighttime tarpon. I put out a second bait. This time, I went with a small slip sinker rig to get the bait down to the bottom, since we weren't seeing any rolling fish. It wasn't long before the bait on the bottom became very active, so I passed the rod to my girlfriend and reeled in the other bait. I was watching her rod closely when I saw the tip dip down suddenly, and before I could say anything, she screamed, "I got one!" In an instant, the line began screaming off the reel. During the day, when we were preparing the gear and talking strategy, I had emphasized the importance of bowing your rod to a jumping tarpon, and as she fought the fish, I could see her line in the shimmering light start to rise. "He is coming up," I yelled out, and as the fish came out of the water, she skillfully bent over at the waist, pointing the rod tip directly at the fish like she had done it a hundred times before. The mighty fish shook its head violently from side to side, trying everything to throw the hook. Again and again, he jumped, and each time, you could hear his gill plates rattle. The splash, as he went back into the water, sounded like a waterfall! It wasn't long before we had the fish up to the beach, and I waded out up to my knees and grabbed the leader guiding the fish in. We took a couple of pictures, and then I removed the hook and started reviving the fish, moving him back and forth to push water over his gills. Tarpon exhaust themselves during these battles, so it is very important to make sure they swim away under their own power. We released the tarpon and hugged each other with the satisfaction of knowing we had accomplished what we set out to do.

*All prices in this chapter are based on research done just prior to this book's publication. *

4

UPPER AND MIDDLE KEYS

UPPER KEYS

We are going to start off in the Upper Keys. First, as far as I am concerned, the best time to take a fishing trip is whenever you can, so with that in mind, the Keys offer you year-round opportunities to catch your Grand Slam. For the Upper Keys, the season begins as the water starts to warm, somewhere around the end of February. Florida Bay stays active all year, but you will see the number of fish increasing as the water warms up. With these warmer conditions, you will see all three of our target species start to move onto the flats. Tarpon will also be in the channels where live baits are effective. Pilchards, pinfish, and most of all mullet will be your best bet in the channels. Tarpon are actively feeding during tidal swings, so check your tide charts and be out there when the water is moving. Of course, if you are fishing with a guide, they will put you on the best spots.

Key Largo is the longest Key in the chain and is home to Florida Bay and the Everglades National Park. This area has been fished by pretty much every guide in the Keys and is known for bigger bones. Everglades National Park is a spectacular area to fish, with an abundance of wildlife to see on your trip. The mangrove forests are filled with birdlife, including pelicans, egrets, herons, ibis, and the roseate spoonbill. Bird watching, along with the fishing, makes for a great day, especially if you have kids. You may even get to see an endangered manatee! Biscayne Bay, only a short run to the north, really opens up the fishing opportunities out of Key Largo. This huge bay runs from Miami all the way down to North Key Largo and is a great place to catch your Slam.

The first area you want to look at is just north of Small Pumpkin Key and south of Broad Key. There is a series of creeks here that wind their way through Angelfish, Palo Alto, Linderman, and Broad Key that are navigable and have great habitats for all three of our target species. To the west of Broad Key, extending all the way past Palo Alto Key, is a beautiful, large flat that, on the right tide, holds good numbers of bonefish. Broad Creek is a wide channel on the north side of Broad Key that takes you from the Atlantic near Old Rhodes Bank back into and through Cutter Bank. There are lots of opportunities throughout this area.

If you are out on your own (or you can ask your guide), Boca Chita Key is a great little stop on your Biscayne Bay adventure.

The iconic, sixty-five-foot-tall Boca Chita Lighthouse and campground is a great stop for lunch during your day. There is a lot of water to explore here, so make sure you take the time to do so. You will be rewarded. The best bait for bonefish is live shrimp, which you can get at pretty much any bait and tackle store. The same is true for small blue crabs, which are best for permit. Tarpon baits vary, but the most productive are live mullet, followed by live pinfish and large pilchards. Check in with the local tackle store to see what type of artificials and flies are working for the areas you want to fish.

Tavernier is a little deeper into Florida Bay and is a slow-paced, quiet area to spend a fishing trip. Home to the largest inside dry storage marina in the Florida Keys, the Tavernier Creek Marina offers up a variety of amenities, including a dive shop, a tackle shop, a Cuban Cafe, boat rentals and sales, boat detailing, and, of course, backcountry guided trips! It is truly a one-stop fishing adventure center. The skiff ride through Tavernier Creek to Cowpens Cut, into the clear waters off Plantation Key to fish the surrounding flats, is spectacular and worth the trip on its own.

Farther to the west, along the Cross Bank, there is a large flat that extends from the western end of the bank to Carl Ross Key and has a diverse number of banks, drop-offs, ledges, grassy bottom, sandy bottom, and small channels. These provide the perfect setup for bones and permit. A little bit further to the west are the Whipray Keys and Whipray Bas in This location puts you very close to the edge of the Everglades National Park. Here, you will find very productive tarpon waters. This is a large area with some deep spots and channels that, on the right tide, will give you the chance at good numbers of tarpon. The backcountry behind Tavernier and Plantation Keys has beautiful emerald green waters with lots of small Keys to explore. Extending all the way west to the park makes for a memorable day of fishing in this area.

Islamorada is a mecca for light tackle and fly-fishing anglers. "The Fishing Capital of the World" is one of the most sought-after fishing destinations, with unparalleled opportunities to catch a Grand Slam. Boasting quick access to both the Atlantic side and the Gulf, this location ensures that you will maximize your time on the water. Some of the top guides in Florida and legends of the sport of fishing operate out of Islamorada. The stories originating here are legendary, and so are the fishing achievements. There is one guide here who has logged over 800 Grand Slams for his clients! From groundbreaking techniques to catching swordfish in the daytime offshore to the size of hooks used to catch tarpon, Islamorada is at the forefront of fishing development.

On the Gulf side of the isle, you are in the heart of Florida Bay, so your chances of catching tarpon go up substantially. If you have trailered your own boat down and are fishing on your own, you should be able to find plenty of open space to fish. The best baits for bones and permit are shrimp and crabs. You can throw the same for tarpon if you see them on the flats or at least shallower water. If you are fly fishing, patterns that mimic these baits are, of course, your best bet. Stop into one of the local tackle shops on the island to get recommendations as to which patterns are working best at the time of your trip. Islamorada has great fishing, both in the backcountry and on the Atlantic side.

Tackle-busting tarpon can be found on the oceanside of Islamorada. The Windley Harbor leads you out through the Whale Harbor Channel. Here, you will find four other channels surrounded by flats where oceanside tarpon cruise on a regular basis. Of course, the Gulf side of the island is world-renowned for sight fishing for Grand Slams and is where poling the flats in backcountry skiffs was developed. The guides that work out of Islamorada, as you would expect, know this backcountry better than anyone and can put you on the fish. The history of Islamorada fishing permeates the air here, so get down there and enjoy. Book one of these top guides for your best chance to catch a Slam.

Timing

For the Upper Keys—from Key Largo to Islamorada— here is when fishing is best for our three species:

- Bonefish: late February through September, with peak in June. Permit: March through August, with peak in March (Permit spawn in May, moving offshore), Tarpon: March through September, with peak in June and July

Guides

There are so many great guides in the Keys and a lot of different ways to find and book them. For the sake of fairness, I am going to recommend guides who are members of the two governing bodies (The Florida Keys Fishing Guides Association and the Lower Keys Guides Association) for fishing captains in the Keys. All members of these two wonderful organizations are committed to conservation and practice conservation through stewardship. They have made huge commitments to the industry and hold the highest standards of ethics. They all hold a USCG Captain's License and are experts in marine safety. I recommend going to each organization's website and doing research on the guides in the area you will be fishing. Here are a few guides I am familiar with and recommend:

- Captain Joe Gonzalez for Biscayne Bay and Everglades
- Captain Lincoln Rodriguez for Biscayne Bay and Florida Bay

Captain Kerry Wingo for Key Largo

- Captain Duane Baker for Key Largo
- Captain Adam DeBruin for Tavernier
- Captain Jared Raskob for Islamorada
- Captain Rob Fordyce for Islamorada
- Captain Bou Bosso for Islamorada
-

These are just recommendations. Some of these captains may be fully booked, but I'm sure they will be able to refer you to someone else if they are not available.

MIDDLE KEYS

The Middle Keys range from Lower Matecumbe Key to Marathon and have the closest proximity to the Gulf of Mexico of all the Keys. The fishing traffic here is not as heavy as in other, more popular areas, giving you a great opportunity to catch your Grand Slam here. Home to the Hawks Cay Resort on Duck Key, this stretch of the Keys offers you isolation along with prime fishing waters. The resort offers a complete package for those looking to find an all-encompassing location. Once you arrive, it's hard to find a reason to leave the property. It has a beautiful saltwater lagoon, relaxing pool area, spa and wellness center, swimming with dolphins, onsite photography services, multiple dining options, and, of course, access to some of the best backcountry fishing in the Middle Keys. There is a canal that surrounds the property and has fun snapper fishing as well. If you are bringing your own boat down, the resort has an 85-slip marina with all the amenities you would expect from a world-class resort.

Close by, you will find some nice flats around Toms Harbor Keys that are worth checking out. They are heavily fished due to their proximity to the island, but they are worth a stop for tarpon. On the Gulf side, just behind the resort, is Channel Key, which offers you great opportunities for permit and bonefish. The Seven Mile Bridge is just a short run from the resort as well. The Duck Key Scenic Area has a wonderful fishing bridge crossing the Toms Harbor Cut that has great snapper, jack, and grouper fishing, if you want to fill the cooler for tacos and sandwiches! The Keys here lead more to the west than the south, making for some amazing sunsets. So, if you are traveling with kids, or just with your significant other, make time to take in some of the most beautiful sunsets you will ever see.

Marathon is the fishing epicenter for the Middle Keys and one of the most fishing-friendly locales for people bringing their own boats, with over 1200 wet slips available. With numerous marinas and easy access to both the Gulf and Atlantic, Key Vaca Cut acts as a main artery for getting back and forth from both bodies of water on the North end of the island. Marathon's fishing heritage and "Old Keys" lifestyle and traditions attract visitors all year long. The island is known for its private waterfront vacation homes, beachside inns, and tropical family-style resorts that really give you a true Keys experience.

Marathon is full of old salts that are more than willing to bend your ear over a cold beer in one of the many adult drinking establishments on the island. If you are so inclined, I recommend you venture out to find some of these guys, who are very friendly and can share with you some of the rich fishing history of the island. You will learn a thing or two! A little hidden secret awaits you on Marathon as well. Sombrero Beach is a secluded beach on the Atlantic side that is also a turtle nesting site. From April through October, it is not unusual to see Loggerhead Turtles coming onto the beach at night to lay their eggs. During active turtle nesting season, the city limits human activities in the vicinity of the egg sites.

The Middle Keys, and specifically Marathon, offer you year-round opportunities to catch your Slam. Water and wind conditions are good most of the year, giving Marathon consistently good fishing all year. Summer gets hot. Thunderstorms can pop up in an instant in the Middle Keys, but they are usually short-lived. Your guides have a variety of options outside of Marathon. The local waters offer great opportunities and easily allow you to get in a full day of fishing, but Marathon has other options as well. The flats on the oceanside just West of Vaca Key Cut are pristine and, although very close to the island, offer you a large area to fish, minutes from the docks. The Seven Mile Bridge and Bahia Honda are also only a short run from Marathon, giving you even more opportunities!

Timing

In the Middle Keys, the seasons for catching all three species are similar to the Upper Keys:

- Bonefish: early March through October, with peak in June
- Permit: March through September, with peak in March-April or June-September (spawn in May)
- Tarpon: late February through September, with peak palolo worm hatch late in May- early June

Guides

- Captain Mike O'Dell
- Captain Derek Rust
- Captain Scott Yetter
- Captain Dustin Huff

5

LOWER KEYS

The Lower Keys, from Big Pine Key to Key West, is personally my favorite area to fish in the Keys. I mentioned this earlier, but it bears repeating—this area is so beautiful it can literally take your breath away. When you cross the Seven Mile Bridge, you are crossing into the subtropical Lower Keys. Here, the water changes color from emerald-green to turquoise and is "gin clear" in areas that allow for some of the best sight fishing in the world. When the wind is flat and calm in the Lower Keys, sometimes it is impossible to discern the horizon line, and the small islands in the backcountry seem to be floating as the sky is reflected in the calm waters! The pace of life slows even further when you are in the Lower Keys. "Keys Fever" is a real thing down there, and you will certainly get that feeling everywhere except on the water. Although there is a lot of down time while fishing this backcountry, the marine activity surrounding you keeps you on your toes all day.

Sharks, rays, turtles, barracuda, and bottlenose dolphin will keep your eyes and mind busy as you scan the flats for your targeted species. Polling your skiff across the flats is a quiet, peaceful way to hunt for tarpon, permit, and bonefish. It was invented in the keys. Standing on the casting platform gives you a sense of peace, as you block out everything that is going on in your life except what is in front of you in the tranquil water. If you have ever done any trout fishing on a mountain stream, alone with only your fly rod, searching for the pockets that are holding fish, and trying to put your fly in just the right spot, you understand what this is like. Total concentration and focus give you the opportunity to put your bait or lure in just the right place to induce a strike. That is only the beginning though. The fish you are going after are smart and powerful and will truly test your mettle and nerves. There are so many factors working against you to accomplish your goal, but persistence and perseverance will get you there. Work with your guide, listen to what they are telling you, and practice so your casting becomes second nature— whether you are using spin tackle or fly gear. You will only have a limited number of opportunities with each species on your trip, so make sure you are ready physically and mentally when those opportunities present themselves.

BIG PINE KEY

Big Pine Key is a family-friendly destination that has more houses to rent and Airbnbs than hotels, which makes for a nice experience. One of the larger Keys in the chain, Big Pine is also home to the protected Key Deer. These deer can be seen throughout the island and are not much bigger than a large dog, measuring 25 to 30 inches at the shoulders. The deer have acclimated to living with humans and can be seen in yards around the island looking for pools of fresh water. They are not afraid of humans (they must know they are protected), but please don't feed them if you encounter them! Across the island, you will see iguanas, exotic birdlife, and alligators. The famous Blue Hole—a freshwater, abandoned rock quarry that was created to provide building materials for Henry Flagler's Overseas Railroad—is a great place to visit and see the wildlife.

Another must-see on Big Pine is the Old Wooden Bridge Guest Cottages and Marina. Established as a fish camp in the 1940s, its rustic waterfront Dade-County pine cabins originally attracted fishermen, kayakers, and others who craved a taste of the Keys from a bygone era. Unfortunately, Hurricane Irma changed all that. With Big Pine taking a direct hit, the camp was devastated. When the water receded, seven of the old cabins and a two-story office and apartment could not be saved. Today, Old Wooden Bridge is busier than ever, with more rooms available. This is thanks to the addition of a cluster of little houseboats that now fill the marina. Old Wooden Bridge Resort reopened in early 2018, starting with two houseboats. Now, there are 13 houseboats, along with six land cabins, and a dozen power boats that can be rented. Just up the street from the resort, is the iconic No Name Pub that was built in 1936. It has been an off-the-beaten-path favorite of Keys visitors for decades, with its wooden beams covered in signed dollar bills—some say are worth over 90,000!

The camp is located at the base of the No Name Bridge, which, undoubtedly, hosts some of the best bridge fishing in the Keys. Spanning Bogie Channel, the night fishing here for tarpon is excellent. The marina has a boat ramp, boat rentals, and kayaks. It is a quiet, laid-back, and family-friendly place to stay away from the hustle and bustle. The property has been renovated since the hurricane and now offers Aqualodges in addition to cabins.

The fishing off Big Pine is fantastic, with Bogie Channel as a main thoroughfare between the backcountry and Spanish Harbor. You will find numerous flats and channels that offer plenty of opportunities to catch a Slam. Legendary angler Stu Apte fished an area here known as Loggerhead for years and years in relative solitude, and that opportunity still exists today on Big Pine. The oceanside fishing for tarpon here is incredible. Every year from May through July, the tarpon train rolls along the beaches. Visually stunning flats hold large numbers of tarpon and some monster permit as well. Opportunities to see thousands of tarpon in a day are possible this time of year! The ocean side fish are tough, but with patience and persistence, you can catch these migrating fish.

The backcountry of Big Pine is expansive and will give you so many different chances to catch many bones and permit on any given day. Deeper channels like Big Spanish Channel and

Harbor Channel are surrounded by pristine flats, the color and clarity of which you cannot imagine, giving you one of the most beautiful areas to fish in the Lower Keys. For bait fishermen, the usual suspects of shrimp and crab are best. For artificials, patterns that match these baits are key to getting bites. Visit Lower Keys Bait and Tackle right on the Overseas Highway to get caught up on what has been working before you head out on the water, and as they say, "come in as a customer and leave as a friend."

Timing

The seasons for catching tarpon, bonefish, and permit on Big Pine are similar to those of Marathon. The big tarpon migration starts in late February, and the season goes through July. However, there are resident tarpon here all year long, making this one of the best tarpon fisheries in the Keys. Bonefish and permit are year-round as well, but there are peak seasons. Remember, permit spawn in May, so that is a low month for those numbers. Check with your guide as to what they feel would be the best time for you to book a trip, based on your priorities. If your focus is to catch a big permit, they may suggest a certain time of year. On the other hand, their suggested timing might differ if you want to catch a big tarpon. In general, here are the best times for each species on Big Pine Key:

- Bonefish: all year with peak in September through November
- Permit: all year with peak in March, April, and June through October
- Tarpon: all year with peak in March through June

Guides

Here is a list of guides that I recommend based on Big Pine:

- Captain Chris Wilson
- Captain Justin Bachert
- Captain Ryan Phinney

TORCH KEYS

Little Torch Key, Middle Torch Key, and Big Torch Key make up a chain that reaches far into the Gulf below Big Pine Key. They separate the Pine Channel and the Niles Channel, which are two of the larger channels in the Lower Keys, and as you can imagine, they serve as superhighways during the tarpon migration. Large schools pass through this area and can be seen "daisy chaining" in the deeper water and on the surrounding flats. "Daisy chaining" is the colloquial name for when a group of fish bump, rub against, and follow each other around in a constant circle or wheel. Many believe that this is an act of courtship or spawning, during which the females eject eggs that are fertilized by the males. However, scientists maintain that no spawning is taking place. Tarpon larvae are rarely found where this behavior occurs, and studies have turned up no roe or milt nearby. Daisy chaining is just one of this creature's mysteries. Compared to many other species of fish, not much is known about them. This is largely because the tarpon has almost no commercial food value and has therefore warranted far less study than its more nutritious cousins.

While some tarpon are known to remain near the shore all year round, most adult fish make their way out to sea in the late summer, overwintering somewhere in the Atlantic or, in some cases, negotiating the Panama Canal into the Pacific. Their behavior once there, including their spawning activity, remains a bit of a blur, but at some point during this time, eggs are laid and hatch to become tiny, eel-like larvae about 15mm long. These larvae eventually develop into young fish, which make their way back to shallower coastal waters, estuaries, rivers, and creeks.

Even if it isn't an act of spawning, the "daisy chain" may still be a mating ritual. Although I know of no studies into the sexes of the protagonists, so for all I know, maybe they're all girls! They certainly seem preoccupied, but it isn't uncommon to hook a fish from the daisy chain, so don't be disheartened if you come upon a "daisy chain," and at first, they don't seem interested, just keep at it. In any case, target the fish that are circling toward you not away from you, and that will increase your odds of getting a take.

On these two channels, you are likely to see other boats, especially on the weekends, so if you are bringing your own boat down, be sure to practice proper fishing etiquette and be respectful by keeping your distance from other boats. The Keys' shallow water habitats are on the verge of being loved to death by a lot of people new to our waters. A bit of education and etiquette can go a long way toward conservation and harmony. Record numbers of visitors to the Keys who are unfamiliar with navigating the shallow waters of the backcountry are wreaking havoc on vital flats habitats. Most visiting anglers are too often unaware of on-the-water etiquette, right-of-way rules, and navigation markers, which creates safety issues while simultaneously infuriating other anglers. If you are out on your own and see other boats anchored in a channel, they are most likely fishing for tarpon, especially during the migration months. Proper etiquette and common courtesy dictate that you give them a wide berth. If you must go past them, do so at an idle to avoid spooking any fish they might be on. If you approach a flat that you are interested in fishing and there are other boats there, a minimum of 100 yards between you and them is proper etiquette. So, just be aware of your surroundings and give each other some space. There is room for us all.

In the area west of Big Torch Key, you will pass Water Key and Racoon Key. A large basin sits between these two islands. There are a few deeper cuts in this basin that hold large numbers of fish. Then, farther west is Content Passage that takes you out to the Gulf through two small clusters of Keys that are surrounded by sandy and grassy flats. It can get very windy on these westernmost flats that are especially prone to the stronger winds from the Gulf. Your guide will do their best to position you to give you a downwind shot, but you should be prepared to shoot one low or to utilize a backhand cast. Remember, these fish can move quickly, especially when they are actively chasing bait, so casting into the wind may be your best option. In order to prepare for these trips, I try to practice casting in my yard during different windy conditions. Preparation is key to success once you are on the water. Putting in some time at home will help to hone your skills and give you the confidence you need to get your bait or fly in the right spot when the opportunity arrives.

There are a lot of Airbnb and Vrbo options on Little Torch Key, offering a wonderful family experience. The island is a slow-paced environment with very friendly residents. There is a very exclusive resort nearby, Little Palm Island, which is accessible only by float plane or by boat. The dining options are amazing, and if you can get a reservation, it is well worth the expense.

As we go further south from Big Pine to Key West, the fishing seasons become very consistent, so I won't spend any more time on that. The only variable is the weather. When the water cools down due to storms, the flats' action slows down for our target species. Although these changes in weather will affect the bonefish and permit fishing, it does open the flats for different species.

Barracuda fishing can be very fun during these cooler periods. A lot of fishermen do not target barracuda for various reasons, but they are an exciting fish to catch. Like our three target species, you can sight fish for barracuda as well. Spin casting brightly colored tube lures with a wire leader is probably the most common and productive way to entice barracudas. Spotting a 'cuda, casting the lure in front of them, and then retrieving the lure as fast as possible, sometimes right to the boat, will trigger a vicious strike from these toothy predators. The strike is usually followed by a scorching run with several jumps initially, and then you settle in for a tug-of-war! It is not unusual for a barracuda to make several long runs mixed with a few jumps during a fight. As you probably know, these tough fish have very large and sharp teeth, so be very careful handling them at the boat!

Targeting jack crevalle, redfish, and snook during these off-season weather breaks can be a lot of fun. The shark fishing is good too! Blacktips, lemon, nurse, bonnethead, and bull sharks all offer an excellent chance to challenge your skills. Blacktips and spinner sharks are almost one in the same and, once hooked, put on a spectacular show, going to the air over and over while spinning wildly. It is quite the experience to hook a 100 lb torpedo that can burn off three hundred yards of line in a flash. So, don't let a little foul weather keep you off the water.

Your guide will let you know if it is not safe to be on the water, or you can check in with the local marina or tackle shop to see what they say.

Timing

For Little Torch and its sisters, the seasons are just like that of Big Pine:

- Bonefish: all year, with peak in September through November
- Permit: all year with peak in March, April, and June through October
- Tarpon: all year, with peak in March through June

Guides

Guides that fish this area come from different locations, but most are close by. One resident Captain of Little Torch is:

- Captain Brandon Sharp

Others nearby include:

- Captain Justin Rea
- Captain Mike Weinhofer
- Captain Dexter Simmons
- Captain Steve Hancock

CUDJOE KEY

Ramrod Key, Summerland Key, and Cudjoe Key make up the next leg of our journey to catch a Grand Slam. This stretch of the Keys is anchored on the Gulf side by Kemp Channel, which runs from the west side of Summerland Key and the east side of Cudjoe Key, all the way to the Atlantic side. This is a very productive area with lots of workable flats, along with several cuts, making for prime Grand Slam fishing. There is also bridge fishing over the Niles Channel, between Ramrod and Summerland Key, which is very popular with the locals. If you have time, walk out on the bridge, and talk with some of the locals to see what's biting and maybe get some tips.

This area took a direct hit from Hurricane Irma. The category four storm caused severe damage with sustained wind speeds of 130 miles per hour. A ten-foot storm surge swept across this stretch of the Keys, leaving 625 homes with minor damage, 52 with major damage, and 81 were completely destroyed on Cudjoe Key alone. Now, everything is back to normal, and the fisheries in this area are producing well, I am happy to say.

While driving down the Overseas Highway, I'm sure you saw several signs advertising "hammocks." In the Keys, you not only have the kind of rest you can find but also the wooded hammocks on the interior of the islands. These hammocks are areas of dense hardwoods that create a canopy that acts as a habitat for many local species of birds, reptiles, and other wildlife like the Florida Key Deer. Cudjoe Key is home to the

Spoonbill Wildlife Preserve, which is a protected hammock that is home to a large colony of Roseate Spoonbills. Here you will see some interesting understory trees— blackbeads, white indigoberry, the stoppers, and torchwood. One often smells the fragrant, puffy, round, white or pink flowers of the blackbeads before they are seen. The white indigoberry has fragrant flowers and thorny branches, but what makes this plant unique is the white berry with its indigo pulp that can be used as an ink or dye. Spanish stopper and other stoppers were used as a treatment for diarrhea. Thus, the name. White stoppers sometimes emit a skunk-like odor, a phenomenon for which the "how and why" is still unknown to scientists. One useful understory tree is the torchwood, a member of the citrus family and the larval host for the federally designated endangered Schaus' swallowtail butterfly. Torchwoods contain highly volatile oils, making them very flammable and therefore a good fuel. While this tree is protected from harvest today, historically it was used to make torches and sometimes was burned as incense.

On the Northwest corner of Cudjoe Key, there are wonderful trails that take you through the hammocks, to salt ponds where the spoonbills congregate, offering wonderful photo opportunities. Like the flamingo, the color of this bird is determined by two factors. They feed on crustaceans such as shrimp, and this helps give their feathers the pink coloration. Age is another determining factor in their coloring. The older they are, the darker their feathers are. These wading birds are gregarious and are often spotted with other species of birds. They typically feed in the early morning or late afternoon hours. They can be viewed walking through the water, heads down, beaks moving back and forth through the water in search of food. Once shrimp, fish, frog, or other food item is detected, their broad flat bill snaps shut. The prey is captured and then swallowed whole. As beautiful as their foliage is, the same cannot be said for their voices. This Florida bird produces a series of low, grunting, almost staccato-like sounds, similar to "taddataddata." The emitted sounds are rapid and machine-gun-like in succession, followed by a few bars or rounds of what sounds like heavy breathing. Fortunately, spoonbills tend to be relatively quiet birds and are usually only heard during breeding season.

These are also amazing birds to watch in flight. Unlike heron and other wading birds, they keep their legs and necks completely outstretched and you can almost feel the air move around you as they go by. Their large powerful wings swoosh through the air, punctuated by a glide and followed by more swooshing. Also, in the hammocks, you will find a variety of iguanas that are uniquely beautiful but are an invasive species in Florida. They were brought into Florida in the sixties through the pet trade industry, and since their population has exploded, they have become a nuisance to populated areas. Although unique, they can cause a lot of problems for homeowners. They use their clawed feet to dig up landscaping and climb up fruit trees to get food, causing lots of damage and expense to the homeowners.

Cudjoe Key is a sleepy little island that doesn't get much fishing traffic, making for prime opportunities to catch your Slam. With two major channels on each side of the island, numerous flats, and Cudjoe Basin, you could spend a week here easily and not cover half the fishing area. There is a public boat ramp on the north side of the island that is very popular with kayak fishermen. It puts you right in the middle of Kemp Channel, in the heart of some of the best fishing areas. If you are taking your own boat, be very cautious in this area. Cudjoe Basin, on the far western side of the island, is a large basin with numerous flats that can be very productive. This area has some of the most pristine water I have ever seen, and on the far west end of the basin is a cluster of small islands. They sit right on the edge of the Gulf of Mexico. Riding and Sawyer Keys will take your breath away. In this area, sight fishing for bones is one of the purest forms of our sport. It is quiet and peaceful with only the sounds of birds and the gentle lapping of water.

The ocean side of Cudjoe Key is equally beautiful. Making the run out of Bow Channel towards the
Atlantic, you will pass by colorful reefs, which are great for snorkeling. You will see all types of reef fish, lobster, rays, eels, sharks, and more. This area is home to Looe Key Reef, a protected marine sanctuary that is one of the premier snorkel and dive spots in the Keys. On the way out, you will pass Lois

Key, which has three cuts on its North side. With the surrounding flats, they are definitely worth spending some time on.

Timing

For Cudjoe Key, the seasons are just as they are on Little Torch:

- Bonefish: all year, with peak in September through November
- Permit: all year with peak in March, April, and June through October
- Tarpon: all year, with peak in March through June

Guides

Guides for Cudjoe also come from other areas, but there are a few resident guides:

- Captain Andrew Tipler - Cudjoe Key
- Captain Luke Kelly - Cudjoe Key
- Captain Pat Bracher - Cudjoe Key

Other guides serving Cudjoe:

- Captain Bo Sellers
- Captain Nathaniel Sampson
- Captain Bob Paulson

SUGARLOAF KEY

Sugarloaf Key is a U-shaped island that comprises Upper and Lower Sugarloaf Keys. Surrounding Upper Sugarloaf Sound on the east side of the Overseas Highway and opening up to the massive Turkey Basin on the Gulf side, this Key has one of the most diverse marine habitats in the Keys. Not only is the marine habitat diverse on Sugarloaf, but so is its rich history.

Sugarloaf's name has been debated over time. Some say that the name comes from a Native American mound on the east side of Upper Sugarloaf Key. One reason that the island was named is that north of the present highway was said to look like an old-fashioned loaf of sugar. Or perhaps it takes its name from the variety of pineapple called "sugarloaf" that was once grown in the area. These pineapples are soft and don't travel very well, so they are not commercially grown any longer.

In 1850, the census revealed the first three residents of Sugarloaf Key. Those three men were: Jonathan Thompson, a 60-year-old planter; James Anderson, a 70-year-old mariner; and Robert Johnson, a 23-year-old mariner. Jonathon Thompson was known as "Happy Jack." There is a small Key, Happy Jack Key, nearby named for him. Happy Jack was one of a group of men who wandered throughout the Keys, living wherever and however they were able. Others of the group were Paddy Whack, Jolly Whack, Red Jim, Lame Bill, and Old Gilbert. However different their names and varying dispositions, they all united in a common love. The men were entranced by the "fragrant goddess" of whiskey and spent quite a bit of time in Key West, but Jack was always disinclined to the world. Key West probably did not elevate his opinion of human nature. So, he settled himself permanently on Sugarloaf Key and bent his energies to trapping deer and raising fruit. His solitude is not so uncompromising, though, for the crowds of spongers and fishermen that swarm around all the Keys gave him sufficient company, some said more than he deserves. Happy Jack died less than two years after the census article came out from wounds suffered after tripping over an anti-deer gun while he was out walking his farming property. Local deer had been a problem for farming on the Lower Keys, and tripwire guns had been rigged along the paths of the deer. Happy Jack's farm was on Bow Channel and north of the SR-4A and the railroad crossings.

In more modern history, the sponging industry was growing and expanding from Key West, which attracted real estate investor Richter Clyde Perky. The 1920s Florida Land Boom was booming, and Perky saw Sugarloaf as a vacation paradise. He also had real estate investments in the Upper Keys. In the meantime, he hired Fred Johnson of Key West as superintendent to continue the sponge experiments. State Road 4-A became a reality in 1928, but the road passed three miles away on the southern shore. He subsidized Monroe County to build a road (today called Sugarloaf Boulevard) to connect his paradise with the highway. With better access to Sugarloaf, Perky built the Perky Lodge to attract visitors to this new vacation paradise, but there was one problem: mosquitoes! Subtropical climate conditions in the Keys create a perfect environment for mosquitoes, and Perky realized this issue would affect his ability to keep visitors from returning to his lodge, so he put into action a plan. Perky got plans from Dr. Charles Campbell of San Antonio, Texas, who allegedly had seven bat towers in Texas. Johnson, who called it the "bat motel," said there were bats in the Keys at that time. Perky also purchased sex-scented bat guano from Dr. Campbell. Johnson said the smell was awful, and they stayed away from there, and so did the bats. There is an unsupported story that Perky brought in 1,000 bats from New Jersey along with a caretaker named Plutonium Pratt. The story goes that the Key West High School band awaited the bats to awake at sunset. At sunset, the bats awoke, flew off, and never returned. The bat tower stood as a landmark and was registered as a Historic Place on the National Register of Historic Places in 2010. Unfortunately, the bat tower was destroyed by Hurricane Irma in 2017.

The Sugarloaf Lodge is now located on the property and continues to provide visitors to Sugarloaf Key a true Lower Keys experience. With a wonderful restaurant and bar, 31 rooms with waterfront views of Lower Sugarloaf Sound, and private balconies, the Lodge is a great place to stay. There is also a marina right on site with direct access to some of the best fishing and fishing guides in the Keys!

My Experience

As I mentioned before, a lot of my formative years were spent on Sugarloaf Key. Some of my best memories in life are centered around my time fishing the waters around Sugarloaf. I have been fortunate enough to put in years of time in the backcountry and ocean fisheries here, and I am blessed to have had a father who was dedicated to fishing here with his family. One of my earliest memories is the summer of 1974. My father and I made the drive down to the Keys from our home in Virginia Beach to fish the tarpon migration with Capt. Tim Carlile. I always enjoyed the long drive down, and we would break it up into a few days to take in some of the sights along the way. It was a great time with my father, and we would spend hours talking about fishing and what to expect. These talks with my father were gold. We would get each other fired up, challenging each other as to who would catch the biggest tarpon, who would be the first to catch a permit, or who could catch the most bonefish in a day. We would go on for hours, laughing the long drive away!

When we arrived in Sugarloaf, we would always stop by the marina to check and see how the fishing was. My father would catch up with the marina managers, and I would run up and down the dock looking at the mangrove snappers, pinfish, and barracudas that filled the canal. We usually waited for the guides to come in, so we could see what was caught that day and make our plans for the next day. I was fourteen years old at the time, and I remember sitting on the bench outside of the marina for hours as the men would talk about what happened on the water. I would be riveted to their stories, absorbing every bit of knowledge I could, so when I was fishing, I would be ready. The sun-tanned, grizzled captains would spin their stories of great catches and heartbreaking moments on the water as they enjoyed their beers with the visiting anglers. I remember thinking how cool that was and couldn't wait for the time I could share a beer with them. As the sun would set, we would reluctantly leave the docks and marina to get settled for the night. I was never able to sleep from the anticipation of the next day. The tarpon run was on, and the chances of us seeing good numbers of tarpon were really good.

In the morning, we would have a hasty breakfast in order to get down to the marina early and make the most of the day. We stayed at the lodge, so it was just a short walk to the marina. Just like the evening before, we would meet the other visiting anglers, of whom there were only a few, at the bench and talk about the fishing as the captains readied their boats. Pushing off the dock was, and still is, one of the most exciting times of the day for me. Once off, Capt. Tim would reach out to shake hands and look into your eyes, saying, "Let's have a good day, men!"

One day, we were going to target the tarpon coming in from the ocean side as they worked their way to the backcountry. We left the marina and took a right turn to the Harris Gap Channel (a small channel for which you have to idle your boat and duck your head under the bridge as you go), which opens up to the flats of Upper Sugarloaf Sound. The wind was dead calm, and as we got into deeper water, Capt. Tim pointed the skiff toward Tarpon Creek. We head across the sound, seemingly floating across the glassy water.

Tarpon Creek is a serpentine waterway that winds its way through the dense mangroves of the eastern side of Upper Sugarloaf Key. The passage through the creek is a breathtaking ride under the hands of a skilled captain who has known these waters his whole life. Capt. Tim ran this creek with the throttle wide open, making for a white-knuckle ride going through hairpin turns and past very shallow sand banks known to rip the prop off an engine. We zipped past egrets, herons, and pelicans as we navigated the mangrove roots. We slowed down as we approached the end of the passageway because it ends on the flats that parallel Bow Channel. (If you venture out to this area in your own boat, I certainly recommend going very slowly through here!)

We slowly made our way across the flats, scanning the channel in the distance. The quiet of the morning, coupled with the still calm winds, made for an intense anticipation for the day. As we slowly motored along the edge of the deep turquoise channel, we approached a spot where the channel was split by a flat and then reconverged just about fifty yards ahead of us. Here, Capt. Tim told me to drop the anchor. I slowly lowered it into the calm water so as not to make any noise, and as soon as it hit bottom, it tightened up and quickly set. The skiff slowly turned in the current, so the stern of the boat was now pointing out to the ocean. We were perfectly positioned to see fish heading in toward the flats, and our anticipation was so thick you could cut it with a knife. All we needed was for the Silver King to join the party.

After a few minutes of scanning the water for fish, we put out two baited rods—one for each of us, my father and me. This was in the early seventies, and at that time, conventional tackle was the choice for chasing big tarpon. We were fishing medium-weight fiberglass rods with Penn 4/0 reels, star drags, and 30lb monofilament line. Archaic for the tackle of today, it was good, sturdy equipment for that time. Tim had set the baits about fifty feet behind the boat, and we could see them clearly just below the surface. As he began to chum the area, there was hardly any talk on the boat. The conditions were perfect, and it was just a matter of time.

"Here they come," Capt. Tim said. Behind the boat, we could see a chain of tarpon coming about 100 feet away. Just then, they rolled, and we could see that the fish approaching the port side of the skiff, where my father's bait was, were very large. His mullet grew agitated as the fish approached. In an instant, it took off, jumping out of the water as a big tarpon came up from beneath and engulfed the bait in a flash. My father's line went tight as he leaned back and set the hook. The fish took off, leaping into the air, shaking its head with gill plates rattling, breaking the calm, quiet morning, and trying to throw the hook.

"That's a big fish," said Capt. Tim.

"Damn right!" my father responded. Once again, the fish took to the air, this time successfully dislodging the hook and swimming off free. The score was one to nothing in favor of the tarpon.

We quickly reset and went back to the task at hand. We talked about that first attempt and determined we did everything right. He just shook the hook—it happens. The sun was getting higher in the sky, and a gentle breeze started to blow, creating a little texture on the surface of the crystal-clear water. Without warning, my father's rod bent suddenly, and the line began to peel off the reel. We hadn't seen any tarpon, so we weren't sure what we had.

"I think it is a big jack," said Capt. Tim, but as my father picked up the rod and began to reel, things changed.

He said, "It feels heavy," and just then, the water erupted with a monster tarpon!

He took off on a long run, and as he did, Dad settled into his seat, ready for a long fight. The fish moved out of the channel and went on to the flats, where we got our first good look at him. Tim estimated the fish to be well over 100 lb, possibly around 120, which is a large migratory fish. The fish continued across the flat, going for shorter bursts of speed with more frequency, and as the line cut through the water, it created a high-pitched sound and a trail of bubbles that caught the attention of a barracuda. Before we could even think, he bit the line and cut the fish off. The score sat at two-nothing, in favor of the tarpon.

Frustration doesn't come close to describing how we were all feeling. As a teenager, I was getting a little upset that my bait was still swimming around and not getting any attention. So, I said to Captain Tim, in a smart-ass teenager tone, "My mullet stinks."

"Yes, it does, but it is fine as bait," he retorted to put me in my place. So, it was back to work again. We still saw fish, so we wasted no time in getting a new bait back out. Tim had obviously settled us on a tarpon superhighway, so it wasn't long before Dad's bait started darting back and forth erratically. BAM! Another big tarpon jumped out of the water with the mullet visible in its mouth, and my father grabbed the rod out of the holder. He reared back with the rod to set the hook, but the fish hadn't swallowed the bait, and without resistance, he crashed to the deck, landing on his rear. "Damn it," he screamed in frustration, and as he got himself up, he looked at me and said, "Next one is yours no matter what." The score was three to nothing, tarpon.

It was on! The fish were there, the conditions were perfect, I had both rods, and the anticipation was palpable for the whole boat. My father desperately wanted me to get a tarpon. My original bait was still swimming along like a stealth superhero on the starboard side of the boat closest to the flat, almost taunting me. I stared him down, willing him to be eaten, but as I was focusing my energy on him, my father yelled at me, "he's on the other bait!" I looked over and could see another big tarpon stalking the fresh bait. I quickly moved to the other side of the boat and took the rod out of the holder. I pointed it at the bait, creating slack so it could swim more freely. The chase was on, and as the tarpon rushed up, the mullet jumped out of the water, narrowly escaping the gaping jaws of its pursuer. The big fish chased the mullet down again and, in a slashing leap, grabbed the bait and turned toward the bottom. The pressure of the fish's weight was immediate, and I leaned back hard to set the hook. I felt a solid set, and then the fish took off.

Standing in the stern of the boat, we watched the fish tear off 200 yards of line. Since I only had 300 yards of line on the reel, Tim sprinted to the bow, quickly brought up the anchor, and raced back to the center console. He started the engine, punched the throttle, and took off after the fish. My dad had me by the waist at this point and kept me in check, reminding me to reel. We slowly started gaining back line, and as I reeled as fast as possible, the inside of my arm pushed up against the star drag, burning me because it had gotten so hot from the long run. I still have the scar. Now at the mouth of Bow Channel (the last marker before the Atlantic), the fish made its first jump. It came out of the water next to the marker and jumped as high as the marker itself! It crashed back into the water, displacing as much water as a Volkswagen and sounding like an explosion.

"Wow, that is a monster!" yelled my father.

"It sure is," echoed Tim, "keep him tight, Tee." I continued to reel with all my might, and we were making progress on the fish. He continued to make a series of jumps, turning toward the flats, and eventually made his way onto the flat. We were now about 45 minutes into the fight, and I sat down to finish it. The fish was pulling the skiff across the flat with ease. We could see a wake coming off its back and its powerful tail swinging back and forth effortlessly. Every now and then, he would take a gulp of air and take off in a small burst. The fish maintained a consistent distance of about 100 yards while we battled it out like boxers.

About an hour and fifteen minutes into the fight, two cormorants flew low across the flat between the fish and the boat, heading right for the line. One hit the line, but it held strong. As we all exhaled, the battle continued. I was tired, and every muscle in my body was stretched to its maximum. However, I knew the IGFA rules state that no one can touch the rod, reel, or line during the fight until the fish is brought to the boat. So, I persevered, summoning all my energy to keep up the fight. This fish was bigger than me, much bigger, and my dad kept encouraging me. We had the fish in shallow water and had stuck through the long runs, jumps, birds, and exhaustion so far. I dug deep and stood back up to get better fighting angles on the fish. In about 15 minutes, we had the fish close, and it was almost as long as the skiff itself. Capt. Tim estimated the fish at 125 lb That is an incredible catch for a fourteen-year-old, but we were not done yet—not even close.

Back in the seventies, before current guidelines were put in place, it was common to capture your fish for certification and mounting. So, as we kept getting closer to getting the fish boatside, my father asked Tim where the gaff was on the boat. Well, Capt. Tim Carlisle was known as a prankster, and in a nervous laugh, he said, "yeh...a gaff, where did I put the gaff" as he looked around the boat.

My father was not entertained and repeated, "Tim, where is the gaff?"

He responded, "I think I forgot something."

"Shit!" my dad said.

I jumped in, "I've got him at the boat guys." Capt. Tim went up to the bow scupper and pulled out a sand anchor, which is a series of bent rebar rods welded to a steel shaft. As I continued to put pressure on the fish, he was able to get his hand on the leader and turn the fish toward the boat. He raised his other hand above his head and brought the sand anchor down in a mighty blow. One of the rebar rods penetrated the fish just above the gill plate—one of the toughest parts of the fish. The fish thrusted itself out of the water, shook, twisted, and with a powerful jump was off. I felt the weight of the fish on the line again as it ran off across the flat. The fish had actually straightened out the rebar rod!

An hour and a half into this struggle, we were all at our peak focus and intensity to win this one. Capt. Tim planned for the next time we got the fish up to the boat. When we got him alongside the boat, Tim was going to leader him and get him by the head. Then, my father was going to grab him by the tail. The big fish was only about 50 yards away after escaping the "gaffing" and was visibly tired, so I was putting the pressure on him as best I could. My whole body was aching from the battle, and my forearms were burning and starting to cramp.

"Hang in there, son," my father said, "You've got him. Just bear down and let's bring him in now!"

With that encouragement, I asked for some water, and after a quick drink, I turned toward the magnificent fish and whispered, "Ok, this is over." I leaned back with all my might, turning his head toward the boat.

"Reel, reel, reel!" Capt. Tim yelled, and I just put my head down and started cranking as hard as I could. By the time I looked up again, he was reaching for the leader again, and Dad was positioned to grab the fish's tail. "Ok, I've got the leader. Once I turn him, grab his tail!" Tim barked out his order. He pulled the leader hand over hand until the fish was right up alongside the boat. Then, he reached down, put his hand in the fish's mouth, and grabbed its gill plate. "Got'em!" he yelled.

"Now grab his tail!" My father reached down and grabbed his tail. My instincts kicked in, and I put down the rod and rushed to the side of the boat. As soon as I got over, Tim and Dad lifted the huge fish over the rail and right on top of me! I wrapped my arms around the fish and just held on in pure joy.

"We got him," I screamed out. "We got him!"

After high fives and hugs, we all sat down, exhausted from the hour and forty-five-minute battle, and just stared at the magnificent fish. "He is over 125lbs," Tim said as we all just kept staring at this beautiful creature. "This could be a junior state record. Let's get back to the marina and get him weighed." With that, we secured the fish and tackle and slowly worked our way across the flat and back to Bow Channel. The ride back to the marina was a blur. All I remember was dad sitting beside me with his arm around me, telling me how proud he was of me. The fish took up over half of the skiff! As we pulled up to the marina, the few people who were there came out to the dockside. It was obvious we had a big fish to weigh. Someone on the dock's edge yelled out, "Who got him?"

My father yelled back, "My boy right here!" as he raised my arm up with great pride. It was at that time that I realized how much my body was shaking from the exhausting battle. We pulled the boat up to the dock by the steps near the scale as the marina manager came out to do the official weigh-in and verification. Tim and Dad carried the fish from the boat to the scale, and as they lifted him up, everyone started applauding. I felt so happy and proud. The marina manager was moving the weights on the scale back and forth as people started yelling out their guesses.

As the scales balanced out, the manager gave the official weight as 131lbs and 6 ounces! Afterwards, the fish was taken down and put in the freezer to await an official from Marathon who would verify the catch. Everyone at the marina gathered on the bench, and it was finally my turn to tell a story. As Capt. Tim addressed everyone about the catch and introduced me to speak. Out of the corner of my eye, I saw my father walking up to the group with a six-pack of beer. He handed one to Tim, one to the manager, one to another one of the captains, and finally turned to hand me a beer, saying, "Son, you deserve this beer. I am so proud of you." With that, we all raised our beers, and I began to speak. As a nervous 14-year-old boy, words were hard to come by at first, but then recounting the fight with everyone leaning in made it easy to speak. We stayed around for a couple of hours participating in this age-old ritual that continues to this day. Father and sons, captains and marina managers, and new friends with old, sharing stories that everyone will remember and pass on.

Not only can Sugarloaf give you the chance to catch big tarpon, but a Grand Slam is a very real possibility as well. The expansive area, which is part of the Great White Heron National Wildlife Refuge in the backcountry, is rife with bonefish and permit flats. The guides that fish these waters know this area very well and when each flat will turn based on the tides. If you are going it on your own, time and patience will be the key here. This area is so big and offers up so many different fishing options, your biggest obstacle will be deciding what you want to fish for first!

On the far side of the basin, at the edge of the Gulf, are the Barracuda Keys. This remote area is a bit of a run from the marina at Sugarloaf, but it is well worth the ride. As I mentioned in the Cudjoe section, this area of the backcountry is remote and beautiful like no other place. There are several cuts surrounded by flats that will give you good chances for bonefish and permit. Johnston Key Channel, on the east side of the Barracuda Keys, is a large, deep channel that separates Turkey Basin from Cudjoe Basin. It is not uncommon to see large numbers of tarpon in this channel, but be warned, the water rips through here and is very tide dependent. It passes through the middle of the Great White Heron National Wildlife Refuge near two of the larger Keys in the Barracudas and will give you a chance to see a variety of birdlife that inhabit this protected area year-round. There is also a very good chance you will see the resident Atlantic Bottlenose Dolphin.

Once again, for bait fishermen, shrimp and crab are your best bet, and artificials that have a matching pattern of these baits are best for fly fishermen or spin tackle guys and gals. While you are on the waters surrounding Sugarloaf, whether you are with a guide or on your own, take the time to really absorb your surroundings. This remote part of the Keys is truly spectacular, and I know if you really take the time to breathe it in, you will be wanting to come back time and time aga in

Timing

For Sugarloaf Key, the seasons are just as they are Cudjoe Key:

- Bonefish: all year, with peak in September through November
- Permit: all year with peak in March, April, and June through October
- Tarpon: all year, with peak in March through June

Guides

Guides for Sugarloaf are:

- Captain Tim Carlile
- Captain Will Benson
- Captain Doug Kilpatrick
- Captain Justin Rea

KEY WEST

Key West is the most well-known and the furthermost inhabited Key in the chain. It boasts a rich history of fishing, and stories of epic battles fought here with blue water monsters are legendary, thanks to Ernest Hemingway. Anglers coming to this area are spoiled with the opportunities that await them. The

Atlantic serves up marlin, sailfish, tuna, dolphin, wahoo, kingfish, grouper, snapper, and many more species to entice fishermen out on the water. It is as diverse as you will find anywhere, with bonefish, tarpon, permit, redfish, snook, barracuda, jacks, and a variety of sharks giving anglers any challenge they want. Key West, however, is not a sleepy hamlet like some of the other Keys we have visited on this adventure. So, it provides families and those looking for a little more entertainment a great way to experience a more upbeat trip.

There are numerous places to visit downtown during the day, and it boasts one of the most world-renowned nightlife scenes you can find. For families, there are beach activities, with Smathers Beach the best public beach for kids. It boasts a sandy shoreline and tame waters, as well as public bathrooms, food concessions, and rentable gear for snorkeling, kayaking, and other water sports. The snorkeling here is quite good for a centrally located beach. The Key West Butterfly and Nature Conservancy is a must-see for kids, with hundreds of living butterflies and colorful birds that will keep the kids well entertained. Taking the Conch Train Tour is a great way to see all the sites along the main drag of Duval Street, which also gives the adults a chance to plan out a little nightlife fun for themselves. The train takes you through the heart of the nightlife district. A few of my personal favorites will give you a taste of old school Key West with a mix of a modern-day experience.

On the corner of Duval and Green St. is the iconic Sloppy Joe's Bar, which was founded in 1933. The bar went through a couple of name changes during prohibition and was finally settled in 1937. Hemingway made this place famous, as he struck up a long-term friendship with the owner Joe Russell. Russell was a charter boat captain, rumrunner, Hemingway's boat pilot, and the author's fishing companion for twelve years. In his company, Hemingway once caught an astonishing 54 marlin in 115 days. Hemingway called Joe "Josie Grunts" and used him as the model for Freddy, the owner of Freddy's Bar and captain of the Queen Conch, in *To Have and Have Not*.

A relatively new saloon near Mallory Square is the Hog's Breath Saloon. It has some of the best music in the Keys as well as traveling entertainers who visit all year long. The saloon also hosts a 5K fun race, which is great fun for the family. Willy T's is right in the middle of Duval Street and is a nice respite from the hustle and bustle. They are famous for having live music all the time, and the food is well worth the stop.

The Rum Bar is a nice change of pace from the rowdy bars of Duval Street. Here, you will feel at home sipping a classic cocktail or one of their 350-plus rums from all over the world. Rum flights consisting of five shots are available starting at $25. The bartenders specialize in traditional rum drinks, of course, but their house specialty, the "Painkiller," has become legendary on the island.

One last must stop is the Green Parrot Bar, which was established in 1890 and is a true watering hole steeped in Key West tradition. If the walls could talk, this is the place you would want to hear. This piece of history is home to a rugged and ragged group of some of the friendliest people on the island. They are famous for divorce parties, tattoo contests, pet birthday celebrations, and fundraising events. The Parrot started as a grocery store for Cuban and Bahamian transplants who brought their rice, beans, rum, cigars, and infectious Latin rhythms in through the grocery backroom. Here, local musicians created impromptu descargas or jam sessions.

When World War II started, the grocery store became The Brown Derby Bar. It was a bunker-like hangout for sailors from the submarine station only a block away on the base. It has been quite a shock for those sailors from the fifties and sixties to see how much Key West has changed when they come to visit, but once they get to the "Old Brown Derby," they know they are home.

After the Navy pulled out in the 70s, astute Judy Sullivan decided to transform the space into an open-air hippie, biker, vagabonds, and free spirits watering hole to keep up with the times, and she renamed it The Green Parrot. It became a place for travelers to meet and mingle with the bar's cast of eccentric local characters. Hippies, sailors, and nomads occupied the barstools, telling stories, and every now and then, a celebrity or two could be seen seeking refuge in its cool anonymity.

When the Key West Pink Shrimp were discovered, it turned into a "shit-kickin' fisherman's honky tonk" for the fleet. Along with them came the nefarious "fishermen" who brought contraband from Jamaica and Columbia, along with more cash than they could spend. In 1983, Jim Beam and his wife Linda acquired the bar, and they began a love affair with the sometimes-rowdy corner bar that lasted over thirty years. The Parrot's reputation has not only been built by nights when the bar was packed, and the party spilled onto the streets, but also by the simple acts of its patrons' kindness and compassion to others. The music, raw and powerful, coming from the small stage, helped a bit as well! In 2011, after the relationship with the Beams, partners John Vagnoni and entrepreneur Pat Croce took the reins and have continued the environment of great music and spirit. It remains a place where you can share a beverage and a thought, and a place where anything is possible at any time. It is a place where people can share their stories with no distractions or pretense of a charade. As they say, "a place just to be."

The backcountry of Key West is expansive and has a lot of different areas to target for your Slam. The guides in Key West can take you to a wide variety of fishing grounds, some within a short run and others to remote edges of the fishery. As you leave the docks and head out through the infamous Man of War Harbor, the massive Northwest Channel will be to your left and the Garrison Bight Channel on your right. You will pass
Fleming Key, which is home to the Special Forces Underwater Operations School. There are huge flats bisected by the Calda and Bluefish Channels that give you great fishing options close to the marinas. Exploring these areas on your own will be a great experience with such a large playing field to work with.

Further to the east, in the area north of Stock Island, is a beautiful stretch of the backcountry that is unmatched in its natural beauty. There is a small cluster of dense mangrove-covered Keys, called Cayo Agua, which are surrounded by small channels and cuts with magnificent flats. This beautiful little cluster of islands provides you with more targeted fishing opportunities in comparison to the wide-open expanses to the West. It is also a good place to hide from the wind coming from the north, as well. Similar to Cayo Agua but a bit larger is the Harbor Keys. Made up of Lower, East, and West Harbor Keys, it is fed by surrounding channels and the Gulf. The waters surrounding this chain of Keys are abundant with baitfish. Glass minnows, pilchards, pinfish, and mullet can all be found around the shallow waters and roots of the mangroves, so for bait fishermen, make sure to have your cast net with you.

Keep going East, and you come into Jewfish Basin, which is fed by the large Jewfish Channel—well known for its grouper and cobia fishing. The channel is also a great place to see large schools of permit and usually bigger fish. Deeper into the basin, it is not uncommon to see large daisy chains of tarpon. The flats on each side of the basin are predominantly sand, making for an ideal place to sight fish for bones. So, this area gives you an opportunity to see all three of our target species in very close proximity to each other.

Between Jewfish Channel and the Mud Keys, there are five shallow channels that have beautiful flats between them—an area worth spending time on. The Mud Keys are probably the farthest east you should travel. This cluster of small Keys is a protected Wildlife Management Area and home to roosting frigate birds, nesting osprey, and a small white heron rookery. There are four navigable cuts through the series of islands and two smaller cuts on the far west side that are closed off to boaters. The Mud Keys are a popular area for boaters to visit and enjoy the shallow, tranquil waters. You will probably run into partiers during the weekend if the weather is nice, so be prepared to work your way around these groups. On the Gulf side of these islands, nice flats reach out to the edge of the Gulf of Mexico and have lots of pockets, edges, and drop-offs that hold all three of our target species. It is also a great place to fish if the wind is coming from the east because these flats are protected from the wind.

Timing

The seasons for fishing the areas around Key West are the same as most of the Lower Keys:

- Bonefish: all year, with peak in September through November
- Permit: all year with peak in March, April, and June through October
- Tarpon: all year, with peak in March through June

Guides

Guides for Key West:

- Captain Mike Cyr
- Captain Nicholas LaBadie
- Captain Ian Slater
- Captain Justin Valakis
- Captain Lindsay Harper

6

CONSERVATION

LEADING ASSOCIATIONS

As you plan your trip to the Keys, especially if you are trailering a boat, keep in mind that you are entering one of the world's greatest marine environments. The areas from Biscayne Bay to the Everglades, down through the backcountry and over to the Atlantic side, through all of the "cuts" and flats, into all the channels, basins, and coral reefs, is a sensitive place that is home to countless types of wildlife dependent on its health. As anglers, it is imperative to always practice conservation. Over the years, the Keys have experienced natural disasters, mainly hurricanes, which have altered the fishery, and recently, the cruise ship industry has been called on to lessen its impact on the ecosystem. These resilient waters can heal themselves from a lot of things, but managing our impact falls squarely on our shoulders as anglers. We are the stewards of conservation, and that begins with practicing catch and release—especially with the species we are targeting. There are guidelines put in place by the Florida Keys Fishing Guides Association, the Lower Keys Guides Association, the International Game Fishing Association, and the Bonefish and Tarpon Trust teach us about catch and release practices and how to handle the fish we bring to the boat.

The Florida Keys Fishing Guides Association is a nonprofit organization that has pioneered conservation efforts in the Keys since 1956. Its membership of professional fishing guides is committed to preserving and protecting the fisheries and other natural resources of the Florida Keys and the Everglades. I outlined the history of the organization at the beginning of this book, but I can't emphasize the importance of this group in maintaining the overall health of this great fishery enough. The Lower Keys Guides Association is also a non-profit of professional fishing guides dedicated to working for a sustainable resource through wise management practices. Here is s statement from their website:

> *The Florida Keys are an unparalleled ecosystem. With reefs, wrecks, tidal flats, and mangrove shorelines set amid a staggering arrangement of aquamarine colored waters. It is America's sub-tropical playground welcoming visitors from around the globe. The economy of the Florida Keys (Monroe County) is driven by access to this ecosystem. In a NOAA study it was surmised that upwards of 63% of the County's economy is derived from direct and*

> *indirect use of this resource. Without question, this ecosystem is our community's greatest resource. Yet it is finite. Pressure to accommodate a growing variety of uses and higher volume of users, has resulted in the need for management to protect and ensure that it remains vibrant, and healthy for years to come. It is the task of lawmakers to find a balance between access for users and protecting the health of this ecosystem. We are dedicated to becoming active participants in this process.*

Established in 1997, The Bonefish and Tarpon Trust is an organization dedicated to "conserve and restore bonefish, tarpon, and permit fisheries and habitats through research, stewardship, education, and advocacy." They have collaborated with numerous universities, including my alma mater, to expand their knowledge of the fisheries and educate the public. Shortly after the start of BTT, the organization invited 60 of the "Who's Who" of saltwater flats fishing to form Bonefish and Tarpon Unlimited. Early on, the board started projects to build public awareness and to recruit new members. Its initial research efforts focused on bonefish tagging efforts to track data on population baseline, size, growth, and range of movement. The same was done for tarpon shortly afterwards.

In 2003, BTU held its first Bonefish and Tarpon Research Symposium, bringing together 20 participating scientists, as well as a large group of the public. The symposium is now held every three years and boasts over 35 scientists. In 2009, the organization introduced the *Bonefish and Tarpon Journal*, a bi-annual publication, to provide information on BTT's latest scientific efforts and to understand and conserve bonefish, tarpon, and permit habitats. The Journal also features fishing articles, angler and guide profiles, photographs, and catch & release tips. The Journal is a great read with many interesting articles on conservation. In its latest publication, there are articles that cover the movement and habits of tarpon in the Keys, bonefish pre-spawning aggregations, Bahamas mangrove restoration projects, and the rise of shark predation in the Keys. I highly recommend contributing to BTT and getting your subscription to the Journal.

BEST PRACTICES

I want to point out the current recommendations by these three organizations on fish handling and best practices. Throughout the years, as conservation efforts continue to evolve, the way we handle fish has evolved as well. It is now common practice when using artificial lures or flies to crimp the barb on your hooks and minimize handling times. Reduce the use of circle hooks if you are bait fishing. Have pliers or hemostats at the ready to facilitate a quick removal of the hook. If you are fishing with a guide, he or she will be the first one to handle the fish. Note that they will wet their hands and/or use anti-microbial fishing gloves to handle the fish. You should do the same. Fish secrete a glyco-protein slime from the cells in their skin to make it harder for parasites to attach. Some fish even secrete toxins into the slime to deter predators. Fish scales provide protection and reduce water turbulence. They overlap from head to tail and are only attached at the front edge, so protecting bonefish and tarpon from loss of scales will decrease the chance of post-catch predation. Permit have much smaller scales, so proper handling of them is even more important to ensure their chances of survival upon release.

Although catch & release fishing is a valuable conservation tool that can lead to more and bigger fish in the fishery, it doesn't guarantee that the fish lives to be caught another day. Fight time is also an important piece to the puzzle of catch and release. As for bonefish, a shorter fight time leads to increased survival because the fish is not exhausted, leading to less of a chance of predation. However, bringing in a "green" fish can mean more thrashing about and difficulty handling the fish and its release. Find the right balance between lighter tackle for sport and heavier tackle. It is up to you and your guide to decide how to achieve your Grand Slam while practicing healthy catch-and-release practices. If there are predators in the area, such as sharks and barracuda, it may be best to keep your bonefish in a live well until the threat passes, or you can move to a safe area near the mangroves to release the fish. Make sure the fish has regained equilibrium and is swimming upright to ensure its best chance for survival.

Fight times for tarpon can be much longer than bones or permit, so the time at the boat or beach is important to ensure a safe catch and release. Tarpon are amazing fish that have been around for over 18 million years because of their adaptability. They have developed a "lung-like" air bladder that not only allows them to process oxygen from water but also from air. When you see "rolling" tarpon, that is what they are doing, breathing in air. So, when you are hooked up with a tarpon, every time they come up and gulp air, they are rejuvenating the oxygen levels in their bloodstream, allowing them to fight harder and longer.

If you are lucky enough to catch a tarpon over 40 in, it is very important to keep the fish in the water. These bigger fish exhaust themselves with multiple jumps and long runs, so trying to keep the fight time to thirty to forty minutes is optimal, but often not possible. Keeping the fish in the water is imperative for fish of this size. Tarpon under forty inches should be handled gently and only removed from the water for no more than fifteen seconds. If you are going to handle the fish, only use wet hands and support the fish under the belly and head. Make sure to resuscitate the fish completely until it swims away on its own power.

As I mentioned before, my degree is in photography. Taking photographs of our catches is not only important to us as anglers for preservation's sake, but sharing our photos and stories is important to the growth of the fishing industry. I have many beautiful images on my walls from fishing trips around the world. It has been instilled in me by the guides I work with that handling your fish safely while trying to get the best image must be pre-planned and executed quickly to minimize the time the fish is out of the water. These fish are tough, strong fighters, and they get exhausted (just as you will) during these battles. We need to respect that by having a plan to get your pictures and get them back into the water as quickly as possible.

Talk with your guide while at the dock or with your family before you get out on the water about getting your photographs ahead of time. Things happen fast out on the water. Being prepared with a plan will minimize the impact on the fish while you are trying to get your photos.

Plan out which side of the boat or what angle to the sun you want to be in, and position the photographer accordingly. Once you secure your fish, wet your hands and gently lift the fish out of the water, but leave it over the water. Do not bring the fish in over the boat. This way, if the fish wriggles or jumps out of your hands, it will fall back in the water and not on the hard surface of the deck. This could cause scale damage that is detrimental to the overall health of the fish. Get your pictures quickly, return the fish to the water, and revive it as quickly as possible. You will have beautiful images for your albums, and the fish will live on.

Special note: Mechanical lip gripping devices can damage the mouths of all three species, especially if the fish is "green." These devices can cause jaw and gill damage that can lead to the fish being unable to eat for a long period of time.

7

HABITAT PRESERVATION

One of the most important issues facing conservation in the Keys is habitat preservation and restoration. At this time, our state fisheries are managed by bag limits, seasonal closures, and slot sizes. Even with these management practices, we are still seeing a decline in our recreationally harvested and catch-and-release-only species. The main reason for these declines is loss of habitat, not only in quantity but also in quality. As anglers, it is important for us to advocate for the inclusion of habitat in fisheries management practices.

Florida's coastal habitat has been damaged by development, altered water flows, and pollution. Contaminants running into the watershed, as well as nutrient runoff, have created algae blooms that affect the oxygen levels in the fishery. Sometimes referred to as red tides or brown tides, these algae blooms block light in estuaries, killing seagrasses, shrimp, oysters, and small fish. All of these species are vital to the food chain.

Florida's wetlands have lost approximately 45% of their volume, shrinking the available habitat that supports marine life. Tampa Bay alone has lost nearly 50% of its mangrove forests. In the Indian River lagoon, mosquito ditches and impoundments have had a significant effect on the ability of fish to reach the mangroves. Conditions have also altered the environment that supports oyster reefs, which are a major source of nutrients in the ecosystem. As anglers, we need to be aware of marine habitats when we are on the water. The number of flats in the keys labeled as "severely damaged" by boat props has increased by nearly 90% over the last two decades. If you are taking your own boat down to try for your Grand Slam, familiarize yourself with local topography and bathymetry before you head out to avoid running up on shallow flats.

Remember that the amount of habitat determines the population of each fish species. This means that as habitats are lost, the fish population is lost as well. Of special concern are the habitats that support juvenile fish. Their viability determines whether the adult population thrives. Unlike the adult population, juvenile fish do not have the ability to move from their nursery habitats if they are damaged or degraded. It takes many years for the juveniles to reach the size of adults in the fisheries.

The declining fish habitat has a compounding effect on Florida's economy. Recreational fishing is important, not only because so many of us enjoy the sport, but also because it is the backbone of many regional economies throughout Florida. Healthy fisheries help sustain that.

TARPON HABITAT

The Bonefish and Tarpon Trust has started a program specifically to protect habitats where juvenile tarpon live. The Juvenile Tarpon Habitat Initiative identifies tarpon habitats for protection and restoration. They work with conservation organizations, government agencies, and anglers to protect these habitats. Through education, the initiative is working to promote the value of juvenile tarpon habitats.

As juveniles, tarpon depend on backwater wetlands and swamps for their early development. These are waters that are not fished, but they are essential to the fishery. Many of these bodies of water have been damaged and depleted, forcing the International Union for the Conservation of Nature to classify the tarpon population as "vulnerable."

The majority of juvenile tarpon habitats consist of mangroves, which are essential for coastal ecosystems. They provide critical habitat for many species of gamefish and their predators. This is especially true for the juvenile tarpon, whose life stage depends on healthy, shallow mangrove and marsh habitats. Unfortunately, mangroves are under worldwide threat. Since the amount of available habitat is one of the most important factors in determining population size, the loss of these critical habitats has direct and immediate effects on tarpon, snook, and the fisheries they support.

Juvenile tarpon nursery habitats are likely to be in close approximation to urban areas, which have already caused degradation to these habitats. As coastal populations continue to rise, coastal ecosystems and the fisheries they support are becoming increasingly stressed; therefore, it is becoming increasingly important to protect these habitats.

BONEFISH SPAWNING

Bonefish migration and spawning were first documented in 2011, and since then, we have not only learned more about bonefish spawning but also about their movements and habitat use. Tagging research has demonstrated that bonefish have a small home range. Most tagged bonefish were recaptured within a mile of the original tagging location. Although they spend most of their year on the flats they call home, they travel as much as 70 miles offshore to spawn. When bonefish reach their spawning destination, they gather in large schools called pre-spawning aggregations, and these aggregations can have ten thousand fish! At dusk, the aggregation moves offshore where they dive down hundreds of feet to spawn. After spawning, the bonefish return to their home flats. Some will spawn more than once a season. BTT is working with guides and colleagues to identify pre-spawning aggregations in the Bahamas. They have identified eight locations. Three of these locations were included in new national parks that were designated by the Bahamas National Trust. For the other five, the BTT is working with the Bahamas to develop site-specific protections for these locations.

PROJECT PERMIT

The Lower Keys Guide Association, in conjunction with corporate sponsorship, have started Project Permit to protect permit fishing habitats. Project Permit takes a science-based approach to protecting permit habitats. They support appropriate fisheries regulations and provide the needed information to improve water quality in these habitats. All of which ensure our catch and release permit fisheries remain healthy and productive. Project Permit has funded three separate research studies over the last ten years. A Florida statewide tagging program relies on anglers, guides, and conservationists to tag, release, and recapture permit. This is an animal tracking study, where scientists can track the daily migrations and movements of over 150 permit throughout the Keys and Southern Florida.

Working with the Florida Fish and Wildlife Conservation Commission the Bonefish and Tarpon Trust has established a special Permit Protection Zone encompassing the entire Florida Keys. In this zone, permit harvesting is prohibited during spawning season. The project is also informing habitat protection. Through tracking work, they have identified important flats and spawning sites that drive this Florida Keys fishery. With the information collected and in association with the Florida Keys Fishing Guides Association, they are working with the Florida Keys National Marine Sanctuary to protect permit flats from prop scarring and to protect spawning sites.

Catching a permit is arguably the most challenging and rewarding endeavor in fishing. Although these fish are found around the world, the Florida Keys are well known as the epicenter for catching large permit. Many world records have been caught in the Keys, and their permit fishery and habitat are truly unique in the world. The Florida Keys are the birthplace of permit fishing. Project Permit strives to keep this fishery protected and productive for the future.

8

SHARK DEPREDATION

We have a responsibility to be aware of our surroundings, especially when we are fishing for tarpon, bonefish, and permit. We must do all that we can to keep our catches from predators. Practicing catch and release is great but not if we are going to release our fish only to be eaten by a predator—sharks being the most prolific. Shark depredation is defined as the full or partial removal of a hooked fish by a shark before it is landed. This depredation by sharks is on the increase across the country. The tarpon fishery has been one of the hardest hit by shark depredation in recent years. Bahia Honda Channel has seen a big rise in hammerhead sharks that will take your tarpon, even right at the boat. There are numerous accounts of this

apex predator taking 100 lb plus fish, even after a short fight within feet of the boat. Although exciting to see a shark depredation, it makes life difficult for captains. Unfortunately, with some shark species on the decline, it is not possible to remove the sharks due to their importance in the food chain

In 2019, a Bonefish and Tarpon Trust scientist witnessed, from an observation platform on the Old Railroad Bridge, over 400 tarpon hook-ups throughout the season from 55 boats. Just over 25% of tarpon were caught and released successfully, 15% were eaten while still on the line or just after release, and the rest either spat the hook or broke the line. This type of depredation is being reported across the Keys. With these reports coming in from all over, the BTT did a survey of anglers and guides. Of those who responded (over 400), 77% said they had experienced shark depredation at least once while fishing. Among guides, 75% said that depredation had increased over the last five years, and 87% of them had experienced shark attacks with their clients, resulting in a poor fishing experience. So, it is important for us to help minimize shark depredation while in pursuit of our Grand Slams. The best way to do this is by trying to shorten the time fighting fish. This could mean using heavier tackle and making sure the fish are handled properly. As mentioned before, short

handling times and keeping the fish in the water are two factors that will improve the chance of survival for the fish.

CONCLUSION

I hope you have enjoyed this wonderful trip through the Florida Keys and the quest for a Grand Slam. For those of you who have been dreaming of completing one of fishing's greatest achievements, you are now more prepared to accomplish this feat. Take the information in this book, along with some research of your own, and put it to good use in preparing yourself for the adventure of a lifetime. Whether you are going it alone or including your family, the experiences you will have along the way will undoubtedly leave an indelible impression on your life. Just spending time in this beautiful place, the Florida Keys, will be a fulfilling experience. The rich history of the Keys alone is worth looking into, from the Calusa and Tequesta Indians, to Ponce de Leon, and of course, Henry Flagler. There is no

shortage of interesting subjects to research. Whatever part of the Keys you decide to make your destination, there will be numerous opportunities to discover some of the unique history of the area. I know that your main goal is to catch a Grand Slam, but if you can make the time to meet the local people, enjoy the local cuisine, and take in the amazing scenery, your overall experience will be enhanced.

Having spent so many years in the Keys has given me an appreciation for not only the amazing fishery but also the incredible natural environment. Spending time on the water with your family or while making a new friend in your guide will open a whole new world of discovery. Regardless of the weather, get out and explore. You will be rewarded with a variety of experiences that will enrich your being. Be prepared for anything. Checking in with the local marinas and keeping a consistent eye on the weather forecasts will ensure you have all the information you need to make for a great trip. If your trip is during the summer months, just remember it is hot. Morning and evening fishing trips, even nighttime excursions, are a great way to keep out of the hot, humid conditions. Staying hydrated and wearing protective clothing, along with environmentally safe sunscreen, will ensure that you don't get sunburned. This makes for a much more enjoyable vacation. Fall fishing in the Keys can be

fantastic. It brings both cooler conditions and fewer anglers to compete with. Off-season rates for accommodations also start this time of year. Winter is even cooler but still very pleasant. Although windy days make things tough on the exposed flats, so finding alternative fishing options, like fishing the mangroves for baby tarpon and snappers, may be your only choice. Then, there is the spring fishing season that everyone looks forward to. Things really start to ramp up at the beginning of March. There are several big tournaments that take place during the spring, targeting tarpon, bonefish, and permit. The March Merkin, the Redbone, and the Tarponian Tournament are just a few to investigate. These tournaments feature the best guides and anglers and usually run three to five days.

The Florida Keys have a very special fishing community. Most of the guides that are working today are generational or have been mentored by some of the great pioneering guides of the past. The vast knowledge that is passed down will continue to be shared as time goes by. This will increase the odds for you, as an angler, to be successful. So, keep in mind as you are searching out a guide to fish with, if you can't get a booking with one of the old salts that have been poling the flats for decades, the younger generation of guides have had amazing teachers. Once you start this journey of catching a Grand Slam and you find yourself on the

bow of a flats skiff scanning the water ahead of you with rod in hand, you will quickly feel the pull that has these guides doing what they love. The passion these people show in their work is beyond commitment. Booking your trip with a younger guide gives you both the opportunity to establish a relationship that can potentially last for a very long time. I cannot wait to get back to catch up with the guys and see what has been going on.

For most of us, we only get the opportunity to take a trip like this once a year or even every other year, so the time you spend together will seem very short-lived. Make the most of it by sharing stories and having some laughs along the way. The lives they lead and the things they have experienced have shaped them into worldly beings with a vast understanding of one of the world's greatest marine environments. They have developed a heightened level of skill that affords them the ability to read the winds, tides, water temperatures, light conditions, and habits of some of the most exciting game fish in the world. Guides possess an understanding of what it takes to be patient with beginners and demanding of experts, all the while keeping a clear picture of the task at hand. They have taken up the battle for conservation in a field that is constantly being bombarded with more and more pressure day by day, and have partnered with wonderful organizations to further their cause. These men and women have worked hard with the government to establish guidelines that will help to ensure this vital resource is protected. The anglers of the Keys have the same passions as the guides do, and together they are leading the way to preserve this amazing fishery.

I hope you will draw inspiration from this book. Get to the Florida Keys for some amazing fishing. Make new friendships with the locals, learn from the amazing guides, take in the wonderful natural beauty, and learn more about how you can become part of the ongoing conservation efforts. I hope that you will have as amazing of an experience as the ones I have had. I hope you get to see that daisy chain of tarpon, the glistening tails of a school of bonefish on the flat, and the heart-stopping moment the black forked tail of a permit turns on your bait. Feel the excitement of the hunt and the bond of a mutually respectful relationship with your guide, so that one day, as you are pushing away from the dock, your day will begin with, "Hey, remember that day when we…"

RESOURCES

1. Florida Keys Fishing Guides Association
2. Lower Keys Fishing Guides Association
3. International Game Fish Association
4. The Angling Company
5. Bonefish and Tarpon Trust
6. Florida-keys-vacation.com
7. The Florida Rambler
8. Drowningworms.com
9. Floridakeystreasures.com

ACKNOWLEDGMENTS

I first and foremost want to acknowledge all the captains and guides that call the Florida Keys home and have dedicated themselves to the conservation of the fisheries. They work hard day in and day out to deliver a unique fishing experience to their clients.

I also want to thank Jason Schratwieser, president of the International Game Fish Association, for his guidance.

Thanks also go to Nathaniel Linville from The Angling Company in Key West for taking the time to talk with me about this project and providing me with his extensive knowledge of the subject.

I would also like to thank Captain Tim Carlile for his years of friendship with my entire family and me, and his wonderful wit, which made for some lifelong memories.

Of course, a huge thank you goes to my family for their support, specifically my mother for being a sounding board and my biggest cheerleader.

www.ingramcontent.com/pod-product-compliance
Lightning Source LLC
Chambersburg PA
CBHW020332010526
44119CB00002B/42